A mistit...
is actuall... ...the
disappearance of 1945-79
"good chaps" & their
replacement by rip-off merchants

GOOD CHAPS

(20) "Loss of power corrupts
& absolute loss of power
corrupts absolutely" (Nirad
C. Chandhuri)

(31, 66) Wrongly believes
Tories won 4
elections 2010 - A;
in fact only 2
(they were a
minority after the
2010 & 2017
elections)

(74-6) True Penrose
Desmond affair
of 2019

82-3 Frank Hester or
Diane Abbott

87 'About' 2,600 Russians received British golden visas from 2008 through 2021'

93 The corrupt US Democrat Senator Bob Menendez (now found guilty [July 24])

106 Paul Caruana Galizia
113 (on the Lebedevs)

112 Boris Johnson's late
April 2018 security-detail-
& civil-servant-free
trip to ~~Alex Lebedev~~
in Italy (after the
Skripal poisoning.)

Good Chaps

SIMON KUPER

(on whose foreign
background &
allegiances see 84,
133)

Profile Books

117 Is it true that Aleksandr
Lebedev ~~is~~ sat the "served in
Stalin's cabinet"?!

First published in Great Britain in 2024 by
Profile Books Ltd
29 Cloth Fair
London
ECIA 7JQ
www.profilebooks.com

1 3 5 7 9 10 8 6 4 2

Typeset in Dante by MacGuru Ltd
Printed and bound in Great Britain by
CPI Group (UK) Ltd, Croydon CRO 4YY

A CIP catalogue record for this book is
available from the British Library.

ISBN 978 1 80522 122 7
eISBN 978 1 80522 123 4
Audio ISBN 978 1 80522 275 0

153 Vaughan Gethin's £200k
(which got him the sack
i Wales)

To all Good Chaps (male and female).
There are still plenty of them.

164 "The more corrupt
the state, the more
numerous its laws"
(supposedly TACITUS)

Contents

A WORD IN ADVANCE

*I genuinely believe that the UK is not remotely
a corrupt country and I genuinely think
that our institutions are not corrupt.*

Boris Johnson, prime minister, 2021[1]

This isn't another book about Boris Johnson, and the
problem is much bigger than him, but he did embody
Britain's lurch towards political corruption. (I will call
corruption corruption, instead of using the preferred
British euphemism, 'sleaze'.) Since the day Johnson
walked into Downing Street in 2019 and began looking for donors to pay for new wallpaper, there have
been so many financial scandals in British politics that
even the most diligent corruption-watchers cannot
keep up, as I discovered when I became one.

At one point during Johnson's premiership, I
received an anguished email from Anthony Ojolola, a
Nigerian Briton who left Nigeria for the UK. Ojolola
wrote:

I hate to kick a man when he is in the gutter. But some of us fled countries where such dishonest and cavalier attitude currently being exhibited by the prime minister is de rigueur. None of this is funny. Not in the slightest. And frankly, I would be damned if I kept my mouth shut and see Britain become another Nigeria ... Alexander Boris de Pfeffel Johnson, for once in your life do the right thing and resign. Standards and ethics in high office are that important. For the sake of God, Go!

Anthony Ojolola. Aggrieved Citizen.

His words about Britain becoming 'another Nigeria' startled me. I had never trusted Johnson, but I suppose that like most Britons, I hadn't taken him very seriously. Now I was jolted into realising how his behaviour looked to somebody who had grown up amid corruption. Ojolola understood how badly a state could go wrong. I ran his views by a Russian friend of mine who lives in Britain. Did the Russian see it like that, too? He looked at me as if I was an idiot. Of course he did.

I don't think British politics could ever become nearly as corrupt as Nigeria or Russia. The UK has more guardrails than they do. But I wrote this book because our politics has become more corrupt than it used to be – and because its drift can be stopped.

The World Bank defines corruption as the use of public office for private gain.[2] Sometimes this use is illegal, but often it's perfectly legal. For instance, David Cameron's lobbying for the Greensill Capital firm during the pandemic didn't break any rules. But Cameron was trying to use his former office as prime minister to make a private gain for himself and a dubious business associate, at the expense of the state.

This book asks: what went wrong? I have followed the money that has been pouring into British politics. But I have also tried to understand the changed norms of the ruling class – the way many of its members have come to justify their self-dealing.

Good Chaps isn't a comprehensive overview of modern British political corruption. That would require a multivolume set. It delivers only a modicum of original reporting. I interviewed everyone from party donors to spies, but I've chiefly relied on the findings of others. Britain has lots of first-class investigative journalists. I am not one of them. Much of what I know about British corruption I learned from reading colleagues such as Peter Geoghegan, Carole Cadwalladr, Gabriel Pogrund, Adam Bienkov, Jim Pickard, George Parker, Paul Caruana Galizia, David Conn, Catherine Belton and everyone at *Private Eye*. Merely contemplating Pogrund's output is exhausting and makes me want to go and lie down. Geoghegan's excellent *Democracy For Sale* (2020) is the most authoritative of the very few books on the subject, and I'd urge anyone who wants to learn about political corruption to subscribe to his Substack.

Some of these journalists work for smaller media like *Byline Times* and *Tortoise Media* that don't (yet) get the attention they deserve. They do their work in – and for – a country that has largely stopped trusting journalism, and understandably so, after the years of hacking and decades of partisan propaganda by many newspapers. Britain is a country where circulations and journalists' pay have collapsed, where draconian libel laws impede anyone trying to expose wrongdoing, and where much of the public has become numb to corruption. Often, anti-corruption activists will turn first to journalists, who expose the story – only to find that there is no follow-up from political parties or the law, whereupon the scandal dies.

This brand of serious muckraking journalism is among Britain's enduring strengths. So are the all-party parliamentary select committees that investigate wrongdoing. So is the Good Law Project, which raises money through crowdfunding to bring legal cases against government. Britain still has enough Good Chaps, male and female. They are the heroes of this story.

I've also drawn on the mountain of information on corruption that's freely available, out there, but ignored. What I have tried to do in this short book is pull all the sources together in one place, and interpret them.

Perhaps nothing does more to destroy trust in democracy than the spectacle of politicians looting the state. But I understand that reporting on corruption, as I'm doing here, can have the unintended effect of eroding public trust even further. A book like this one exemplifies a dangerous tendency in journalism: we report on the people who break the rules, not the people who stick to them. Every revelation of wrongdoing chips away at institutions. There is a jagged line that leads from the *Telegraph*'s exposure of the MPs' expenses scandal in 2009 to the vote for Brexit in 2016.

I have tried to counteract the risk of feeding distrust by proposing remedies throughout the book. A lot can be fixed. I don't believe for a moment that Labour is immune from corruption, but the likely change of power after the general election of 4 July is a chance for a reset. Things used to be better, so they can become better again.

1

LIFE AND DEATH OF
THE GOOD CHAP

'You're a good chap, Bingley.'
'So are you, Mulliner.'
'Both good chaps?'
'Both good chaps.'
'Making two in all?' asked Wilmot,
anxious to get this straight.
'That's how I work it out.'
'Yes, two,' agreed Wilmot, ceasing to twiddle his
fingers. 'In fact, you might say both gentlemen.'
'Both gentlemen is correct.'

P. G. Wodehouse, 'The Nodder'[1]

It was in the grounds of Windsor Castle in 1985 that
Clive Priestley, former head of Margaret Thatcher's
efficiency unit, coined the magic expression. At a
gathering sponsored by the Adam Smith Institute,
Priestley was trying to explain to a group of visiting American political appointees from the Reagan

Administration how the British state worked. 'I have a theory,' he said,

> the 'good chaps' theory, which runs like this: in the higher civil service we begin (expensively) by recruiting terribly good chaps. We are terribly lucky because they've chosen to come to us, and it would be rather base to suggest they ought to be trained. If they are really good chaps, they go on getting better good chaps, until finally one of them becomes the very best good chap of all – the Permanent Secretary.

If you're permanent secretary, Priestley went on, 'the last thing you want to do is to put management targets on any of your fellow good chaps ... because that would be infra dig and bad form.'[2] Priestley was trying to explain why Britain's civil service wasn't particularly efficient (in brief: it wasn't trying to be) but what struck the scholar Peter Hennessy, sitting in the audience, was the phrase 'good chaps'. Hennessy eventually expanded it into a total theory of modern British government.[3]

The UK, he came to argue, worked according to 'the Good Chaps' theory of government: the people who ran the country were considered Good Chaps, who didn't need to be bound by rules because they did the right thing instinctively.[4] (In the 1980s there was still only a sprinkling of chap-esses.) Good Chaps obeyed what Hennessy called the 'Whitehall equivalent of the "Code of the Woosters"'.[5] In fact, he wrote, the British constitution was 'a state of mind'.[6]

That's how the country managed to function – almost uniquely among democracies – without a written constitution. (Or at least not one written down in a single document. Hennessy and Andrew Blick point out that much of the UK's constitution 'is of course written down – in places such as Acts of Parliament, parliamentary regulations, judicial decisions and ... various codes'. However, these are weak constraints. Many could be ditched tomorrow by a parliamentary majority, or simply ignored without consequences.)[7]

Admittedly, the British ruling class always included a few Bad Chaps. The country has a long tradition of corruption scandals, now often remembered with nostalgia. Nineteenth-century landowning MPs bribed their constituents in 'rotten boroughs'; Lloyd George, prime minister from 1916 to 1922, set a more or less formal price list for the sale of honours; there was the cash-for-questions scandal of the 1990s, and on, and on. Political corruption will never hit zero in any country.

But on the whole, Priestley was right. In the postwar decades, Britain was mostly ruled by Good

Chaps – a phrase that I'll use in this book in a gender-neutral way. Government was fairly clean. This century, that began to change. Although we haven't fallen from a lost Eden, things have got dirtier.

There is no precise measure of a country's degree of political corruption, but some authoritative observers have signalled a rise in Britain's level. In 2020, the credit rating agency Moody's downgraded the country's credit status, citing, among other reasons, 'the weakening in the UK's institutions and governance'.[8] (The downgrade tends to make it more expensive for the government to borrow.) Then there's Transparency International, the anti-corruption NGO. It collates surveys of business executives and other experts to rank countries by their perceived level of public-sector corruption. As recently as 2017, the UK ranked joint eighth. In Transparency International's league table for 2023, the UK finished twentieth. (Denmark was number one.)[9]

Some establishment figures now describe British governance in the kind of language that would once have been used by revolutionary leftists. John Major (a Good Chap) said Johnson's Conservative government was 'perhaps politically corrupt'. Lord Evans, chair of the Committee on Standards in Public Life and former chief of MI5, warned that the UK could 'slip into being a corrupt country'.[10] When I suggested to a senior former government official that corruption had crept into the system, I was swiftly corrected: 'Corruption has thundered in.'

So who killed the Good Chap?

*

The crazy thing about the Good Chaps theory is that it more or less held true for so long. Its golden age was the forty-year stretch from Neville Chamberlain's radio address on that sunny September morning in 1939 until Thatcher's entry into Downing Street in 1979, quoting St Francis: 'Where there is discord, may we bring harmony.' In my previous book, *Chums: How a Tiny Caste of Oxford Tories Took Over the UK*, I described these decades as an era when Britain was mostly run by posh men who had fought in one or other world war.

These men were Good Chaps, or more precisely, public-service toffs. They had gone through private school and Oxbridge, before becoming senior civil servants, army generals and BBC bosses. Most took their place at the top of the class system for granted, but they had also limped home from war with the belief that politics was a serious business, and that serving the British state – until death, if necessary – was the highest calling.

Even today, you still encounter some public-service toffs dotted around the British state. Many are the descendants of Good Chaps who fought wars and ran colonies. The most famous extant Good Chap, the podcaster Rory Stewart, explains in his auto-biography why he went into politics: 'My father had fought in the war. My grandfather had been a doctor at the creation of the NHS … The only thing that had ever motivated me since I was a small child was the idea of public service.'[11] And as a public-service toff, Stewart assumed that his service would be served at the top end of the state.

Good Chaps tended to gravitate instinctively to the Conservative Party, their ancestral home. However, they weren't very partisan: Labour's chaps had done their bit in the war, too, and even Tory chaps in the 1939–79 era wanted to improve life for the lower orders. The two parties mostly felt they were working in their different ways for a common cause.

Some corruption scholars wonder why there isn't *more* corruption in public life. After all, why not steal from the state to benefit yourself if you can?[12] Good Chaps refrained from stealing largely because of their shared codes. Britain in their era deterred corruption with unspoken guidelines, rather than with vulgar written laws.

Good Chaps liked to say that sunlight was the best disinfectant. (The phrase comes from the American Supreme Court Justice Louis Brandeis.)[13] Trans-parency alone, they thought, was enough to deter corruption. In the postwar decades, any Bad Chaps, or even Good Chaps who slipped up, were practically embarrassed out of office. John Profumo had served in the Northamptonshire Yeomanry in the Second World War, earning an OBE. In 1961, while Conservative secretary of state for war, he began an affair with the dancer and call-girl Christine Keeler, unaware that she was also sleeping with the Soviet assistant naval attaché in London. The brief triangular relationship did no damage to national security, but on 22 March 1963 Profumo lied to the House about it, saying: 'There was no impropriety whatsoever in my acquaintanceship with Miss Keeler.'[14]

When the lie was exposed, he resigned from politics for good. He spent much of the rest of his life doing penance through charitable works, washing dishes and tending to addicts in London's East End. His friend Jim Thompson, the Bishop of Bath and Wells, reported: 'He says he has never known a day since it happened when he has not felt real shame.'[15] Sunlight disinfected Profumo.

True, there was money-grubbing even in the Good Chaps era. Five days after Profumo's false statement to the House, his cabinet colleague Ernest Marples presented the Beeching Report, which would lead to the closing of thousands of Britain's railway stations. Marples, transport minister since 1959, presided over the birth of Britain's motorways. He opened the first one, the section of the M1 between Watford and Rugby. His eagerness to build roads may have had something to do with the fact that he was a road-builder by trade. Only in 1960, under pressure from the Commons, had he sold a large stake in the road-building company Marples Ridgway to an unknown buyer – who probably wasn't his wife, as was rumoured at the time. Marples fled to Monaco in 1975, reportedly to avoid having to pay almost thirty years of overdue tax. He died there in 1978.[16]

Another Conservative contemporary of Marples and Profumo, Reggie Maudling, became a frontman for the Yorkshire architect John Poulson. In 1972, when Poulson went bankrupt and was revealed to be corrupt, Maudling, then home secretary, wrote his own (admittedly obfuscatory) resignation letter over lunch.[17] He was allowed to escape public shaming. The Good Chaps era was less transparent than our own. But Maudling was, metaphorically, locked in a room with a whisky and a revolver and encouraged to do the right thing.

Today's oldest living Good Chaps entered public service in the 1960s. Back then, a senior civil servant could still afford to buy a nice house in London, with enough left over for school fees. At the time, there was little to tempt him away from public service. There wasn't yet much money to be made in the sleepy City of London, where local kids played on the bombsites left over from the Blitz.[18] Few Britons were rich enough to buy politicians. The top rate of tax on 'unearned' income peaked in the 1970s at 98 per cent.[19]

But then came Thatcher, the first British prime minister to have reached adulthood after the world wars, and the tide began to turn against Good Chaps. Admittedly, Thatcher herself didn't countenance self-dealing in office. David Willetts, who joined her Number 10 Policy Unit when he was twenty-eight, told me that the ethos that protected her against corruption was Christianity. The barrister John Bowers recounts in his book *Downward Spiral: Collapsing public standards and how to restore them*: 'Edwina Currie (the former MP) recalls that Margaret Thatcher was so fastidious that when ministers met in Number 10 to talk politics (as opposed to government business) she insisted they chip in a few pounds from their own pockets to pay for sandwiches.'[20] Thatcher believed in public service. Yet she thought that the highest calling for other Britons was business. To get rich became glorious. The Thatcherite ethos made the idea of serving the state for its own sake seem a bit silly.

Thatcher claimed to create wealth. She certainly created more wealthy individuals. She cut taxes for the rich. Her 'Big Bang' of 1986 deregulated the City, turning it into a wealth machine. She also put chunks of the state in private hands. Suddenly there was a plethora of companies that cleaned state hospitals, collected garbage and ran sports centres. Since they lived off government contracts, they began courting politicians, legally or otherwise.

Then, under John Major's premiership, Tory standards visibly slipped. A series of scandals, financial and sexual, peaked in the 'cash-for-questions' affair of 1994: the Harrods owner Mohammed Al-Fayed paid the Conservative MPs Neil Hamilton and Tim Smith £2,000 a pop to ask parliamentary questions on Harrods' behalf.[21] When the story broke, it was considered so disgraceful that Major set up the Committee on Standards in Public Life, which he called his 'ethical workshop'.[22] It endures to this day.

The committee drew up the seven so-called 'Nolan Principles': Selflessness, Integrity, Objectivity, Accountability, Openness, Honesty and Leadership. The principles had reportedly been scribbled down on the back of an envelope by the political scientist professor Anthony King, in a belated attempt to codify Good-Chapness. The principles still apply to every national and local holder of public office, and to countless other state employees, from police through NHS staff to teachers.[23]

'The original Nolan report,' says Peter Riddell, the former Commissioner for Public Appointments, 'was a very British exercise conducted by eminent figures in public life based on hearing the views of other

eminent people without any detailed research.'[24]
In any case, the highfalutin' Nolan Principles were
vague and had no legal force. They were widely
ignored even by the few people able to remember
what they were.

2

SHAMELESS

Private affluence and public squalor.
J. K. Galbraith, American economist,
The Affluent Society (1958)

The book that taught me most about the surge in British political corruption since the 1990s isn't, ostensibly, about Britain at all. *Gambling on Development* by Stefan Dercon, a specialist on Africa at Oxford University, focuses on much poorer countries. Yet reading its insights into ruling elites who loot their states, I kept noticing parallels with what had started to happen in the UK.

Dercon argues that a country tends to develop once its elite strikes a so-called 'development bargain'. The bargain involves elite members agreeing to develop the country, instead of just dividing existing goodies among themselves. The elite of an autocracy can strike a development bargain, and so can a democratic elite. What matters is the elite's choice to develop – its decision that it wants to improve life for ordinariy citizens. Examples of development bargains are China from 1979, India from 1991 and Ethiopia until the recent civil war.

Some time this century, Britain's development bargain broke down. Though Dercon's book doesn't focus on the UK, he does note: 'I wrote it as weekend therapy, when failing as decent/productive development policy advisor to the UK foreign secretary in a toxic government [in 2020–21], so what I saw there was on my mind too.'[1] His book shows that elites who focus on enriching themselves tend to target their country's main natural resource. In Nigeria, Dercon explains, that's oil. In the UK, as I see it, the great natural resource is wealthy international London. The corrupt elite forever promises to diversify the economy away from the natural resource (Britain's latest attempt was branded 'levelling up') but somehow this never happens.

In the UK, the temptation for elite corruption has grown in recent decades partly because the natural resource did: international London kept getting richer, while the rest of the country did not. First, the 'Big Bang' kickstarted the City's growth into a giant global financial centre. Soon afterwards, communism fell. A small group of people, notably in the post-Soviet nations, grabbed the collapsing states' assets for themselves. From the 1990s, many of these people moved to London. They bought the stucco houses in Kensington where the Good Chaps' grandparents had lived. The new arrivals had learned in their home countries the necessity of finding a friendly politician to offer protection – '*krysha*' (literally 'roof'), Russians called it – and they set about doing the same in London.

When they made enquiries around Westminster, they were amazed to discover how cheap chaps were. The joke in cosmopolitan circles was that you could become chummy with the British prime minister for the price of an Italian mayor. And the UK was a country worth buying: it remains the world's sixth biggest economy, and the sixth biggest military spender, with a seat on the UN security council.

British politicians were delighted to meet the billionaires. The size of political donations took off from around 2000 – in the Conservative Party's case, especially from recently arrived Russians who had become British citizens. (See Chapters Four and Five.)

Politicians elsewhere in Europe were less exposed to that kind of temptation. Mark Rutte, Dutch prime minister from 2010 to 2024, throughout almost the entire modern period of Tory rule, never moved into his country's official prime ministerial residence. He cycled to work from his ordinary Hague flat, where he didn't even have a coffee machine, just a steam kettle. It's harder to live like that in political London. Here, if you have a family and you want to be a powerbroker, even if your mission is to do good things, you need a lot of money just to keep going.

The twenty-first-century UK was losing both Good-Chap seriousness, and its state's relative wealth. That made it more vulnerable to corrupters. As the Indian writer Nirad C. Chaudhuri had remarked of Britain decades before: 'Loss of power corrupts, and absolute loss of power corrupts absolutely.'[2]

The UK was a weakened host, unable to resist infection. London was experiencing the emergence of two elites. There was an elite of private affluence in Mayfair and, to a waning degree, the City. Just a limo ride away at Westminster, there was the elite of deepening public squalor. The wealth gap between the two elites widened after 2010, when Conservative austerity slashed the state. Mice scampered through the crumbling House of Commons. Chaps and chapesses in the public sector just kept getting cheaper.

In any generation in London, there are a few clubs or restaurants that serve as meeting-places where state and business elites get acquainted. Today's preeminent venue is 5 Hertford Street, the Mayfair members' club that opened in 2012. 5HS is based in some knocked-together eighteenth-century houses on a cosy little street tucked away behind Shepherd Market. You saunter past the club's doorman, push through a thick velvet curtain, and pass into another

world – though only after the glamorous reception-
ists have verified that you belong there. Inside, 5HS is
like a British gentlemen's club with a touch of Dubai.
In the warren of little sitting-rooms and restaurants,
ministers, celebrities, lords and ladies, lobbyists,
European royals and private bankers drink tea (or
whisky, depending on which lounge and hour of day)
with oligarchs.

5HS's owner, Robin Birley, had been one of the
first Brexiteers. He is the stepson of James Goldsmith,
founder of the Referendum Party, which opposed
the federalist EU. In the 1997 general election, Birley
briefly stood as the party's candidate for Kensington
& Chelsea, before stepping aside to enable the racist
Europhobe Alan Clark to win the seat for the Tories.[3]
Birley retains his old allegiances, and 5 Hertford Street
(or in the phrase of one habituée, '5 Heart of Darkness') is popular with prominent Leavers like Nigel
Farage, Michael Gove and Arron Banks.[4]

Another regular describes 5HS as 'the Brexit sex
dungeon'.[5] Nights here sometimes end downstairs
in Loulou's nightclub, about which the less said, the
better. 5 Hertford Street and its even more exclusive
nearby offshoot, Oswald's, are the updated versions
of the Pall Mall gentlemen's clubs. (The nearby dance
club Annabel's, founded by Birley's father Mark, used
to be an elite gathering spot but now gets mocked as
'nouve'.)

5HS is where Prince Harry and Meghan Markle had their first date. There's a fireplace in every room. Dogs are welcome.[6] The former Conservative minister Nadine Dorries spent many happy hours here writing *The Plot: The Political Assassination of Boris Johnson* (one of the three worst books I have ever read). She recounts her first meeting at the club, in a private sitting-room with a 'bust of a gorilla perched on a windowsill': 'The room was so inviting, so comfortable, so something indistinguishably secure and rooted in Englishness and childhood that I could have sat there forever.'[7]

In 5HS and nearby venues, the Mayfair and City elites began to corrupt the Westminster one. Most British politicians today are not very rich. They tended to have gone straight from university into politics or journalism, where salaries, never spectacular, have stagnated. True, politicians earned far more than the average Briton, but the Tories, in particular, didn't compare themselves with the average Briton. They didn't know the average Briton. They lived in Notting Hill, not Britain, and they measured themselves against their contemporaries from school and Oxford who were making millions as hedge-funders, private bankers and property developers, often by servicing rich foreigners.

Then, in 2016, came Brexit. One of its side-effects was to feed corruption. The leading Brexiters, from

their perch in 5 Hertford Street, believed they spoke
for 'the people'. They regarded the Good Chaps as
an unelected Remainer establishment, 'the Blob' –
the British version of what Turks and Trumpists
(and a growing number of Tories) call 'the deep
state'. Brexiters felt they were fighting a battle for
Britain's independence. Given the stakes, it was fine
to break a few rules (and ignore the uncodified ones)
if that would win a referendum or election. They
should even be able to shut down parliament if it
got bolshy.

Democracy needs defending against certain politicians, but also against certain voters. Many voters
were fine with the rule-breaking of post-Brexit governments, especially if it upset Remainer judges and
journalists. And if some Brexiter politicians did a bit
of thieving along the way, well, everybody was doing
it, and anyway, these thieves were on the side of the
angels. Any watchdogs or judges or biased media
or other blockers who kicked up a fuss were just
Islington-based enemies of the people.

Tory Brexiters joined a nationalist-populist movement that stretched from Trump's US through
Hungary to Israel. Its collective mission, wrote the
Princeton scholar Jan-Werner Müller, was 'captur-
ing the state in the name of "the people"'.[8] This
movement did not accept checks on its power. No
wonder that the *Economist* magazine found that when

a government became more nationalist, its country tended to drop down Transparency International's rankings of perceived corruption.[9]

In 2019, Johnson became the most unabashedly Bad Chap to run Britain since Lloyd George a century earlier. The UK had few rules to stop him. Politicians were allowed to accept presents, and parties could take unlimited donations, as long as they declared them (and then hoped that nobody bothered to read their declarations).

Sunlight was supposed to disinfect. But sunlight didn't bother Johnson. Sunlight doesn't bite. And in the British system, sunlight was supposed to be delivered by the *Sun* and other media. Either they were biased in favour of Johnson, or his supporters dismissed them as biased against him. For all the sunlight, the infection hung on in Downing Street for three years. It only went away when the Tories concluded after Partygate (a scandal that 'cut through' in a way that financial ones didn't) that Johnson had become an electoral liability.

The most common excuse for personal corruption in any society is, 'Everybody does it.' Johnson set the tone for the government. If the man at the top was out for personal gain, anyone lower down would have to be a fool not to do the same.

Johnson came into conflict with the remaining Good Chaps he encountered inside the British polity.

He pushed some of them out of the Tory party. His best-known victim, Rory Stewart, complains that shame has disappeared from British politics. That's not quite right, though. There's still plenty of shame around. It's just that nowadays it attaches itself to different vices than before. We have (rightly) come to consider it shameful for politicians to bully or sexually harass or expose themselves. This change in mores helps explain why more than one in twenty of the MPs elected in 2019 had, by December 2023, left parliament, been suspended or had the party whip removed after misconduct allegations.[10]

Conversely, though, financial venality is no longer considered particularly shameful. That's how Grant Shapps could become defence secretary in 2023, his fifth cabinet post in under a year, despite being known to have used an alias (or possibly several aliases) to sell 'Stinking Rich 3' and other self-help guides on the internet while an MP – something he had spent years denying.[11] A Good Chap would have spent the next few decades washing off his humiliation in some soup kitchen; Shapps seemed unbothered.

*

The costs of political corruption are tangible. Every pound snaffled from the public realm means one pound less to spend on schools, bus stops, hospitals, pensions, benefits and public-sector pay. Corruption kills – just think of the underfunded NHS.

And corruption can infect a whole society. Experts distinguish between 'petty' and 'grand' corruption. Grand corruption means self-dealing by people at the top of the state. Petty corruption means people like doctors, teachers and civil servants charging bribes for things that should be part of their job. While British grand corruption worsens, petty corruption remains almost non-existent outside certain local councils and police forces.[12] In a Eurobarometer survey for the European Commission in 2014, precisely zero per cent of British respondents said they personally knew someone who took bribes. Fewer than 1 per cent said they had been asked or expected to pay a bribe. (Numbers were similar in other north-western European countries, whereas in Lithuania the proportion was 29 per cent.)[13]

But everyday British public life probably won't remain clean if grand corruption becomes endemic. Any system rots from the head. A nurse, civil servant or police officer reading about self-dealing at Westminster could be forgiven for thinking: 'Obviously we're not all in it together. I'll never be able to buy a home, perhaps I'm struggling to feed my kids, I'm earning less than I did in 2010, I'd be a mug not to take anything myself.' Robert Barrington, an expert on corruption at Sussex University, asks: 'Is it possible for there to be a corrupt government and a clean country? Yes – for a while. But it does not last for long. Systemic political corruption always – with no exceptions – opens the door to corruption elsewhere in both the public and private sectors.'[14]

Perhaps most damagingly, corruption eats away at people's trust in politics. 'They're all in it for themselves' is possibly the core message of populists like Nigel Farage, many of whom are in it for themselves.

British voters have always been suspicious of politicians. Even in 1944, when the country was run by men who had volunteered for the front in the First World War, and who were working day and night under German V2s, 35 per cent of Britons told Gallup pollsters that politicians were 'out for themselves'. By 2021, in a poll by the Institute for Public Policy Research, the proportion saying politicians were 'out for themselves' reached 63 per cent, then the highest on record.[15] By December 2023, in a poll by We Think for *Byline Times* asking specifically about politicians in Westminster, it hit 70 per cent. A magnificent 1 per cent of We Think's respondents described Rishi Sunak's government as 'very honest'.[16] Other pollsters have also found trust in politics at an all-time low.[17]

British voters might eventually be tempted by a Trumpian charlatan who promises to 'drain the swamp'. Already, they are unwilling to trust politicians with a mission as expensive and complex as, say, the energy transition. Why wouldn't ministers just use it to funnel contracts to mates and donors? After all, that's what they did at a national life-and-death moment with the Covid VIP lane.

Most Britons have come to expect political corruption. The shock that greeted the MPs' expenses scandal in 2009 is unthinkable today. Ever fewer wrongdoers even seem to get punished. The case study is cash for honours: the illegal practice of politicians handing out peerages as rewards for political donations. In 2006, when Tony Blair was suspected of giving peerages to people who had lent money to the Labour party, he became the first prime minister to be questioned by police, three times.[18] Some Labour figures were arrested. The scandal probably hastened Blair's resignation in 2007.[19]

Yet by the 2020s, cash for honours had become the norm. Anybody whose donations to a political party exceeded a certain sum of money could expect to become Lord or Lady So-and-So. Nobody made a fuss about it anymore. British politicians might envy the sums of money that circulate in American or Brazilian politics, but at least they didn't have to worry about ever being prosecuted. It's not clear anymore just what a PM or minister would need to do to get arrested. In politics, 'we seem to have entered an age of impunity,' remarked Margaret Hodge, the Labour MP who chairs the All-Party Parliamentary Group on Anti-Corruption and Responsible Tax.[20]

The shamelessness is fitting in a country where impunity has spread to all classes of criminals, mostly because austerity slashed law enforcement. The Tories were defunding the police before it was cool, and 43 per cent of courts in England and Wales closed between 2010 and 2024.[21] In 2021, with recorded crime at a twenty-year high, only 5.6 per cent of all offences reported to police even led to a charge or summons, let alone a conviction.[22]

Hodge's remark about impunity reminded me of something. In 2005 I had interviewed Derk Sauer, a Dutchman who had become a media mogul in Moscow. Sauer published dozens of Russian titles, ranging from a local version of *Cosmopolitan* to the financial daily *Vedomosti*. But, he explained,

> In Russia, the effect of what you publish is different from in the West: nothing happens. We reveal something every week: that someone is corrupt, that the justice system has made a mistake, we reveal the craziest things. And nothing happens. Deathly silence. It is revealed that the ballot boxes were rigged in the elections. People just say, 'So you thought the elections weren't fixed?'

Imagine that in a country like Britain, Sauer marvelled back then.

Nearly twenty years later in Britain, corruption

is revealed, and usually, nothing happens. Deathly silence. Few people even notice. Often, a powerbroker who has ripped off the state for millions gets away with it, while the tabloids return to their favourite subject of some poor sod on benefits who has supposedly defrauded the state of several hundred quid.

Andrew Feinstein, a former South African MP who began exposing corruption in his own country, and now runs Shadow World Investigations from London, says: 'In South Africa, in a township, people can discuss details of corruption deals in relative detail. Britons have only a vague sense of what happened with the Covid VIP lane, and so on. I suppose the reason is that for more people in South Africa, it's a matter of life and death. They need a strong and efficient state.'

*

British parties enter the general election of July 2024 better funded than ever before, with an array of individual donors giving millions of quid each to the Tories or Labour.

If Labour win, I expect corruption to decline, for a while at least. That's because 2020s Conservatives seem unusually prone to it. First, Tories tend to admire wealth and distrust regulation, a dangerous combination. Second, their public-service toffs are dying out. Third, Tories are more likely than Labour politicians to have jealousy-inducing rich peers. Fourth, there's that strand of Brexit that encourages rule-breaking.

Fifth, any party that has been in power for too long starts to malfunction. The Tories have gradually attracted the sort of grifters who attach themselves to any seemingly permanent ruling party – see United Russia or South Africa's African National Congress. The Conservatives are now also experiencing the fading of a common project at the fag-end of an era, when many politicians see defeat coming and start looking after number one. It was similar (if less bad) in the dying days of John Major's government.

Lastly, Conservatives, especially after four straight election wins, have developed a tendency to take British voters for granted. Labour is almost always surprised by victory. Its politicians tend to feel they won power through an aberration, are forever under attack from right-wing newspapers, and need to be on their best behaviour. If you're living in your own house, you feel entitled to raid the fridge at midnight; if you're staying in someone else's house, you probably don't.

But we've seen in the past that Labour, too, is perfectly capable of corruption. Rich London is coming to tempt the next ruling party as it did the Tories. To understand how British politics works nowadays, we have to follow the money – and politics is one of the few sectors of the UK economy where there is more money than ever before.

3

THE DONORS HAVE SPOKEN

*The donors have spoken today – some key
people in the Conservative Party that you
will hear about and see over the next hours. A
large number of MPs believe that they should
be listening to their constituencies, and the
prime minister should remain in post.*

Nadine Dorries, culture secretary, arguing for
Boris Johnson's survival in office, 6 June 2022[1]

There are many routes by which wealth corrupts
British politics. But the most direct is the rise in donations to political parties – above all, the Conservatives.
Though big donors rarely feature in the media, and
are less well-known to the public than certain colour-
ful MPs, they are much mightier powerbrokers. The
UK has moved closer than most people realise to the
donor dominance of American politics.

True, British political donations are smaller than in
the US: the $160 million-plus that Ron DeSantis spent
on his prematurely abandoned presidential campaign

was more than all British parties spent between them in 2023.[2] However, the shallower British money pool just means that any individual donor has more influence. There's less competition for access to power here. British parties are desperate for donations. That has made it easy for a small group of rich people to, in effect, buy shares in them.

I've broken up my examination of donors into four chapters. In Chapters Four and Five I'll look at the set of donors who came to London from abroad, especially Russia, retaining worrying ties to their home regimes. These people pose a specific set of threats to British democracy. I'll discuss Labour's donors in Chapter Six.

The current chapter recounts the long rise in party donations, and looks specifically at the native-born donors who give to the Conservatives. Several of these men – and they are almost all men – also funded the Leave campaign in 2016.

*

At the height of the Good Chap era, parties had little need for donations. They got most of their funds from their armies of members. British party membership peaked in the early 1950s, at 2.8 million for the Tories and about 1 million for Labour. If you added in members of trade unions affiliated to Labour, the party's membership hovered somewhere around 5 million from the end of the war until the early 1990s. In many British towns, local party headquarters occupied a fine building on the high street. Lots of apolitical people became members just to have somewhere to play snooker or dance on a Saturday night. (The first gig the adolescent Paul McCartney ever played was at 'a place called the Conservative Club, which was above a shop in Broadway, Liverpool'.)[3] All those concerts, members' fees, raffles and (for Tories) wine-and-cheese evenings funded the political parties. But over the decades, the members died off. By the late 1980s, Tory membership had shrunk to 1 million.[4]

This meant that local parties were going from profit centres to cost centres. Instead of sending funds to party headquarters, they now needed handouts from HQ just to survive. But where was HQ supposed to get the money?

Labour in the 1980s still got most of its funds from the unions, but the Tories under Thatcher needed donations. They turned to big business. The party's treasurer throughout her leadership was Alistair McAlpine, whose great-grandfather, 'Concrete Bob', had founded the family's construction empire. McAlpine would invite company bosses and tax exiles for lunches at the all-male Garrick Club, where they would be expected to cough up to fund more Tory rule.[5] Frightened that Labour would raise their taxes and maybe even renationalise their companies, many obliged. McAlpine was one of the few people Thatcher was always willing to meet one-on-one.

Even in that era, the occasional crook donated. Asil Nadir, a businessman who had given £440,000 to the Tories, flew to his native Northern Cyprus in 1993, disguised in a hat and dark glasses, and celebrating on the plane with champagne and caviar. He was fleeing justice: he had been charged with sixty-six counts of theft after the collapse of his conglomerate, Polly Peck. The Conservative Northern Ireland minister, Michael Mates, had famously given him a watch inscribed, 'Don't let the buggers get you down.'[6] Decades later, Nadir returned to Britain and was jailed in 2012 for stealing up to £29 million of Polly Peck's money. Even after that, the Tories refused to return his donations.[7]

The still greater embarrassment, the one that made almost everyone in politics agree that something must be done about donations, was the Bernie Ecclestone affair. In 1997 the diminutive right-wing Formula One boss, a longstanding Tory donor, gave Tony Blair's Labour £1 million. Soon afterwards, Labour came to power, on a manifesto promising, 'We will clean up politics'.[8] Then Blair pushed to exempt Formula One from the EU's forthcoming ban on tobacco advertising – by a strange coincidence, hours after he had a meeting with Ecclestone.[9]

The story was considered shocking. Blair had to return Ecclestone's money, and make a public apology.[10] More lastingly, Labour was shamed into passing what remains the last significant British law regulating political donations.

The Political Parties, Elections and Referendums Act (PPERA) of 2000 relied on the traditional British disinfectant: sunshine. The Act still let parties accept as many donations or loans as they liked, though it tried to ban ones coming from abroad. The biggest change was that every donation of more than £5,000 had to be declared. (By 2024, the reporting threshold had risen to £11,180.) A new, independent Electoral Commission was set up to oversee donations. People assumed these measures would wean parties off massive gifts like Ecclestone's.

The problem was that parties needed to get money from somewhere, and they weren't getting it from members anymore. As in many other democracies,[11] the long-term collapse in British party membership appeared unstoppable. David Willetts, the former Conservative minister, told me: 'My constituency party in Havant was probably one thousand people when I was first elected in 1992, and probably three hundred when I stood down in 2015.'

By the first decade of the century, the Tory party got only 3.5 per cent of its income from membership fees.[12] The French economist Julia Cagé remarks, in

her book *Le prix de la démocratie,* which compares the
funding of parties in different countries: 'The Conservative Party is not a mass party.'[13] In the long run,
the rise in donations and the fall in membership were
probably mutually reinforcing: as parties sold themselves to the super rich, ordinary people's distrust
of politics grew. The 'sunlight' provided by the new
transparency rules doesn't seem to have disinfected
politics, but merely alerted the public to the role of
money.

Wonks get very excited about their favourite alter-
native to donations: state funding of parties. They
are forever drawing up schemes for taxpayer-funded
'democracy vouchers', which voters could give to
the party of their choice. It's a lovely idea, but it's
not going to happen. As the Lib Dem MP Martin
Horwood testified to the Committee on Standards in
Public Life in 2011:

> In the current context, I do not fancy particu-
> larly going on to the doorstep and explaining to
> people that their libraries are shutting and their
> day care is being closed down and we may not
> be able to put as much on housing benefit as we
> used to, but good news; do not worry, we are
> giving more money to political parties. I think I
> might get a punch in the face.[14]

British public funding for parties is lower than in comparable countries: about £13 million in total in 2022–23, or 25p per registered voter. That compared with about €3.50 in France and €5.50 in Spain, calculates Daniel Chandler of the LSE.[15] Boosting funding by £150 million would take Britain to around the French level. That's politically unthinkable. Yet a donor-free political system could have saved the taxpayer a fortune. To take only the most shocking example: the Covid VIP lane, through which the government handed contracts for protective medical equipment to some useless companies run by Tory donors, wasted billions of pounds.

In real life, the only credible source of funds for British parties was donations. The three main parties understood the risk that donors could corrupt the system. They tried to agree a limit on donations. In 2007 they nearly struck a deal for a cap of £50,000, but negotiations failed.[16] The Conservatives wanted a quid pro quo in the form of a tight cap on Labour's funding from unions, and Labour wasn't keen. The limit in Canada, by the way, is just C\$1,700 (about £1,000) for donations to party or constituency.[17]

In the general election of 2010, all three parties made manifesto commitments to reform party funding.[18] Somehow, the winning Tory–Lib Dem coalition never got around to passing a law. Donations remained unlimited.

Still, the fond British belief persisted that big money in politics was an American problem. When prime minister David Cameron appeared on the US TV talk-show *The Late Show with David Letterman* in 2012, he said, 'We don't allow political parties to advertise on television, so that massively cuts the cost of ...' whereupon the American studio audience interrupted him with an ovation.[19] Americans at the time were steeling themselves for national elections in which the forecast spend on TV advertising was $3 billion. Cameron told the admiring Letterman that he had been allowed to spend just $150,000 on his campaign to become Tory leader in 2005.[20] I remember watching the clip at the time, and feeling the familiar sense of British civilisational superiority over the US. Weren't we Good Chaps?

In fact, Cameron was being disingenuous. It's true that Britain strictly curtails spending in the 365 days ahead of general elections. It has done so since 1883, when a law was passed to rein in out-of-control campaign spending. British candidates in the 1860s and 1870s spent about two hundred times more money per voter in real terms than they do today, even though the country was much poorer then, calculates Cagé. Viewed narrowly, the 1883 law worked. British election spending is now much lower than in France, let alone the US. British donations do peak in election years, when donors are most motivated, but that's not always when the money is spent.[21]

Yet there's a crucial omission in the 1883 law: Britain places no limit on parties' spending *outside* general elections. And that's when they spend most: on permanent party staff, wonks to dream up policies, long-term general-election prep, local election campaigns, videographers, focus-group coordinators, advertising, and on, and on. Anyway, a party can artificially suppress its official election spending by delaying big payments to temporary staff and to pricey campaign consultants like Lynton Crosby and Isaac Levido until the day after the election, when the spending cap is lifted.

The Conservatives have also long received an untold amount of what is in effect free campaign advertising in the form of propaganda in the *Daily Mail*, *Daily Express*, *Sun* and the *Telegraph*. The Tory press – the 'party in the media', as the political scientist Tim Bale calls it[22] – donated, as it were, in kind.

Moreover, by the time Cameron went on Letterman, dedicated election spending was becoming less relevant. Campaigns were moving online. That was a money-saver, because digital campaigns are much cheaper than the old analogue kind, when parties had to print leaflets and buy stamps. (The billboards and the bumf through the letterbox were probably never very effective anyway, and mostly just annoyed voters.) Nowadays, a viral campaign meme can be produced free of charge. In short, British laws on campaign spending miss out on much of what matters in twenty-first-century elections because they were written before social media.

The upshot is that British elections are cheap, especially for Tories. In the 2010 general election, total spend by all parties put together was just £31 million – way below the legal spending limit of £19.5 million per party.[23] In 2019, the major British parties combined spent less than £50 million, whereas American parties and their supporters spent $14 billion on the next year's presidential elections.[24] If by some mishap a local British constituency party exceeded its legal spending limit, the opposing party would often pretend not to notice, knowing that next time it might be the culprit in need of clemency.

All this means that anyone following the money in British politics has to look beyond election campaigns. More and more, parties are spending on their long-term apparatus. And this is increasingly funded by donors.

*

The Tories always had many more committed donors – people who gave even when the party was in opposition – than Labour did. But Tory fundraising reached new heights of ambition from 2003, when the party created a 'Leaders Group' of donors.

The Conservatives' website later promised that the group's members would meet Cameron and 'other senior figures from the Conservative Party at dinners, post-PMQ lunches, drinks receptions, election result events and important campaign launches'.[25]

The way Britain works, some donors in the Cameron era were his schoolfriends.[26] One donor, the venture capitalist Adrian Beecroft, was asked by the party to review employment law. It may astonish you to hear that his report, published in 2012, proposed diluting workers' rights.[27]

Cameron, around the time of his boast to Letterman, was revealed to be hosting parties for funders at his Downing Street flat.[28] Peter Cruddas, then co-treasurer of the Tory party, appeared to have told *Sunday Times* reporters posing as potential donors how much access different levels of donations would buy:

> Two hundred grand to 250 is premier league ... What you would get is, when we talk about your donations the first thing we want to do is get you at the Cameron/Osborne dinners.
>
> You do really pick up a lot of information and when you see the prime minister, you're seeing David Cameron, not the prime minister. But within that room everything is confidential – you can ask him practically any question you want.

> If you're unhappy about something, we will
> listen to you and put it into the policy commit-
> tee at No. 10 – we feed all feedback to the policy
> committee.

When the story broke, Cameron responded: 'This is
not the way that we raise money in the Conservative
Party, it shouldn't have happened. It's quite right that
Peter Cruddas has resigned. I'll make sure there is a
proper party inquiry to make sure this can't happen
again.'[29]

Yet donations have just kept growing since – above
all, to the Tories. To quote the academics Mirko
Draca, Colin Green and Swarnodeep Homroy:
'While Labour Party donations are essentially at the
same level in real terms in 2019 as in 2001, donations
to the Conservative Party grew by multiples of three
to four times over this period.'[30] The Conservatives
have outspent Labour at every general election this
century.[31] By 2019, there were 116 'super donors' in
British politics, defined as individuals giving more
than £100,000 to a party in a single year. A few were
handing over millions. That year, for the first time,
total political donations hit £100 million.[32]

The question then is: who are the donors behind
the country's default ruling party? They are no
longer, as in Thatcher's day, literal 'captains of industry' – bosses of large companies listed on the stock

market. Labour's PPERA Act forced listed companies to get shareholders' approval before making political donations. Few companies even bothered trying. They were replaced by individual donors.

It's not always easy to discover who these individuals are and how much they have donated. Take, for instance, Conservative donor Michael Farmer, a devout Christian and long-time City metals trader known in the markets as 'Mr Copper'. 'The first time I met David Cameron,' Farmer recalled, 'he asked me what was my "thing" in politics. "Families," I said, "the government can and must do more to support family life".'[33] Stuart Wilks-Heeg of Liverpool University found that the registry of political donations lists Farmer's name in five different variants, which don't automatically link to one another, such as Michael Farmer, Michael S. Farmer, Mr Michael S. Farmer and Lord Michael Farmer. (Like many donors, he was, no doubt coincidentally, made a peer). 'Twenty-five different donor IDs have been applied to his donations,' marvels Wilks-Heeg.[34]

Still, even with this kind of confusion, it's possible to draw up some sort of taxonomy of Britain's biggest political donors. Some are old money – heirs to big companies, none of them bigger than the Sainsbury supermarket family. 'The largest private donors to the Conservatives and Labour in the current parliament were both called Lord Sainsbury,' reported my newspaper, the *FT*, in 2023. The Tory peer John Sainsbury (whose final gift to the party was a bequest after his death in 2022) and the Labour peer David Sainsbury are descendants of John James Sainsbury and Mary Ann Staples, who started a dairy shop on Drury Lane in London in 1869. But the Sainsbury cousins were atypical in the ranks of modern political donors. By the time they began giving large sums, they had largely withdrawn from the family business. They were, essentially, rich retirees with political opinions.

This century, a new class of Tory donor has emerged: a small group of rich London-based entrepreneurs, who run their own private companies. These men are property developers, hedge-funders, private-equity tycoons and other City types. And they are entirely atypical of the average British voter.

If there's a catchall phrase to describe these donors, it's 'libertarian buccaneers'. They tend to be impatient with taxes, regulations, Covid-era lockdowns, and 'EU red tape'. Many of them donated to Leave in the Brexit referendum. Some are climate deniers and/or run fossil-fuels companies. Some have agendas that are so idiosyncratic as to be unclassifiable. With others, we just don't know what they want.

A few are flat-out opportunists. The fraudster Peter Virdee, nicknamed 'Batman', sometimes known as Hardip Singh, donated more than £100,000 to the Tories but also gave £2,000 to the constituency party of Labour's shadow international development minister Preet Gill. Virdee, owner of multiple Rolls-Royces, was sentenced to three years and three months in jail in Germany in 2021 for his role in an international VAT fraud. The following paragraphs from *The Times* are so astounding to all but the most hardened students of British political corruption that I had to read them twice:

> 'At times,' the magazine *Spiegel Online* said, 'Singh was one of the most wanted men in Europe.' Posters seeking him were displayed in ports and airports. Marius-Cristian Frunza, an expert witness in financial crime trials ... estimated that part of the money Virdee paid to politicians 'comes from the VAT fraud'.
>
> Both parties carried on taking Virdee's money even after he was arrested by Britain's National Crime Agency on suspicion of bribery and corruption and it told the High Court that he was willing to bribe politicians.
>
> After he became a party donor, Virdee met the Queen and Duke of Edinburgh three times in a year.[35]

There were other spectacular opportunists. Julio Herrera Velutini, a banker from one of Venezuela's richest families, controlled the Britannia Financial Group, which donated over half a million pounds to the Tories. In 2022, US authorities charged him with bribing a former governor of Puerto Rico. He pleaded not guilty.[36] In May 2024 he was awaiting trial.[37]

Separately, Velutini commissioned research from Mark Fullbrook, a senior Tory organiser. Fullbrook said he hadn't broken the law and didn't know that Velutini may have had corrupt motives in hiring him.[38] This story broke in 2022, just as Fullbrook was about to start work as chief of staff to the new prime minister Liz Truss.

Or take the opportunists of Lycamobile, a British telecoms company that was being investigated in France on charges of money laundering and tax fraud. Lycamobile had employed 'three literal bagmen to deposit rucksacks stuffed with millions of pounds in cash at Post Offices all over London', reported Buzzfeed News.[39] In 2017, French authorities asked their British counterparts to gather information by raiding the company's London headquarters. Officials at HMRC told the French that Lycamobile probably wouldn't agree to have its premises searched, and wrote: 'It is of note that they are the biggest corporate donor to the Conservative Party led by Prime Minister Theresa May and donated 1.25m Euros to the Prince Charles Trust in 2012.'

When Buzzfeed inquired about this sentence,

HMRC said: 'We never take political donations into account when working out how to work with other countries, or indeed on our own, in enforcing the tax law.' It explained that the reference to Lycamobile's donations had been included only as 'background' information.[40] In 2023 the company was convicted in France of an 'elaborate money-laundering system'. Two of its executives were jailed for VAT fraud.[41] The story got only a fraction of the coverage of the Polly Peck affair thirty years earlier. Nobody is shocked anymore.

But apolitical chancers on the make are the exception among Britain's donors. Most donors are mixes of opportunist and true believer: they genuinely love right-wing economics, and wish the Conservatives would do more of it, but they also want a personal return on their investment in the party. That return might come in the form of a government contract, or a peerage, or a change to an irritating law, or simply a minister answering their phone call.

Perhaps the biggest beast in the donor pack is Anthony Bamford, a Brexiter who gets around by Ferrari, yacht or private jet. His family company, JCB, founded in 1945, manufactures construction equipment. It's known for its bright yellow diggers. JCB was still supplying equipment for Russian customers months after saying it had 'voluntarily paused' these exports following Putin's invasion of Ukraine in 2022.[42] As of late 2023, HMRC were investigating Bamford's tax affairs.[43]

Officially, of course, Anthony Bamford is Lord Bamford. He's worth about £6.5 billion.[44] His family donates to the Tories through all sorts of entities: various individual Bamfords, and companies such as JCB Services, JCB Excavators, JCB Research, etc. That makes it harder to track their giving. Put together, calculates Wilks-Heeg, they gave the Conservatives over £16 million from 2001 through 2022, making them the party's biggest single donor group.[45] Anthony Bamford also sometimes lent Johnson his private plane.[46]

Another cluster of Tory donors are billionaire hedge-fund managers, or 'hedgies'. Some, by late middle age, get bored with just piling up more money, and decide to fix British politics. After all, they reason, their success in finance proves that they know better than the average voter (and better than the PM) how things work. If only the country could be run like they run their funds.

One prominent hedgie donor is Michael Hintze, who also gives to the Global Warming Policy Foundation, which lobbies against climate science.[47] Hintze, born in China to émigrés from Russia, a former captain in the Australian army, hung a picture of Margaret Thatcher in his office overlooking Trafalgar Square.[48]

Other 'hedgie' donors include Alan Howard, who hired Lady Gaga to sing at his wedding in Italy,[49] and the increasingly influential Paul Marshall, a philanthropist who gives away millions a month to a variety of causes. Marshall, who describes himself as 'a committed Church of England Christian',[50] started out a political liberal. He stood as a parliamentary candidate for the SDP–Liberal Alliance in 1987, later donated to the Lib Dems, but left the party in 2015 after he began pushing for Brexit.

He found a place in the Brexiter elite. In February 2016, Michael Gove called Marshall to get his view on whether he should back Leave. 'It's the right thing to do,' Marshall told him. Months later, when the new prime minister Theresa May appointed Johnson foreign secretary, Gove heard the news over dinner with Justin Welby, Old Etonian Archbishop of Canterbury, at the offices of Marshall's hedge fund, Marshall Wace.[51]

The archbishop had reason to be there. Marshall is one of the biggest philanthropists in the C of E. He pays for the training of a large proportion of its future clergy, and helped fund and create the Church Revitalisation Trust, whose professed aims are 'the evangelisation of the nation, the revitalisation of the Church, the transformation of society'.[52]

One enemy in this crusade, though Marshall doesn't say so in public, appears to be Islam. The anti-racist campaign group Hope Not Hate reported, after an analysis of his protected, anonymised Twitter account: 'Marshall has repeatedly liked and retweeted extremist content from an array of far-right and conspiracy theorist accounts for months, endorsing tweets that call for mass-deportations and suggest a civil war between "native Europeans" and "fake refugee invaders" is imminent.'[53] *Prospect* magazine collated quotes from tweets Marshall had liked or reposted (though he later said he didn't agree with all of them):

- there has never been a country that remained peaceful with a sizeable Islamic presence
- once the Muslims get to 15 to 20 per cent of the population, the current cold civil war will turn hot
- If we want European civilization to survive we need to not just close the borders but start mass expulsions immediately.[54]

A spokesman for Marshall told Hope Not Hate: 'Paul Marshall's account is private but is nonetheless followed by 5,000 people including many journalists. He posts on a wide variety of subjects and those cited represent a small and unrepresentative sample of over 5,000 posts. This sample does not represent his views.

As most X/Twitter users know, it can be a fountain of ideas, but some of it is of uncertain quality and all his posts have now been deleted to avoid any further misunderstanding.[55]

Whatever Marshall's real ideas are, they have influence across the British right. As co-owner of the extravagantly loss-making TV channel GB News,[56] he put Tory politicians right up to Boris Johnson on his payroll.[57] Most strikingly, the Conservative-turned-Reform Party MP Lee Anderson, self-appointed voice of 'the working class', briefly the Tory party's deputy chairman, earned £100,000 in 2023 for presenting a show on GB News. (Just eighteen months earlier, Anderson had chastised fellow MPs: 'If you need an extra £100,000 a year on top then you should really be looking for another job.')[58] In short, Anderson was making more from Marshall than from representing his constituents.

Marshall poured tens of millions of pounds into GB News, but quit its board in April 2024, while remaining as 'a co-lead investor'.[59] The move seemed intended to bolster his bid to buy the *Telegraph* Group newspapers and the right-wing *Spectator* magazine. That would give him an important voice in the direction the Tories take after their expected defeat in the general election.

The Gift of Brexit

The reign of the individual buccaneer Tory donors really starts with the Brexit referendum in 2016. That was the moment when the historical party of British business turned away from mainstream British business (or, in Johnson's phrase, 'Fuck business').

Most companies, especially larger ones, backed Remain in the referendum for economic reasons.[60] Remain's biggest donors included the American banks Goldman Sachs, JP Morgan, Citigroup and Morgan Stanley.[61] But just five buccaneer donors provided the majority of funding for the various Leave campaigns. The most generous donor was insurance entrepreneur Arron Banks, followed by four men who have all at different times been major Tory donors: Crispin Odey, the hedge-funder who in 2023 would be ousted from his own company amid detailed accusations from twenty women of sexual assault and harassment; City financiers Jeremy Hosking and Peter Hargreaves; and the motor-trade entrepreneur, property developer and Evangelical Christian Robert Edmiston. Between them, this quintet accounted for £15 million of the £24.1 million in official donations to Leave campaigns in the five months before the referendum.[62]

Many Leave donors longed for a hard Brexit that would free their businesses from European bureaucracy. Bamford's JCB had been fined €39.6 million by the European Commission in 2000 for anti-trust breaches. JCB declared itself 'very frustrated' after losing a six-year legal fight against the fine.[63]

Marshall accused the European Commission of launching 'an onslaught on hedge funds' after the global financial crisis. Hargreaves had been fulminating against European regulations since at least 1990.[64] This pair and Odey were among the hundred-plus executives from the financial services industry who warned, in a letter released by Vote Leave weeks before the referendum: 'We worry that the EU's approach to regulation now poses a genuine threat to our financial services industry and to the competitiveness of the City of London.'[65] The rising young Conservative Leaver Rishi Sunak, himself a hedge-fund alumnus, held similar views.

The Leave campaigns threw the usual parties where donors mixed with politicians, not always to the donors' benefit. Tim Shipman, in his book on the campaign, describes 'a viewing party for donors thrown by Matthew Elliott in Westminster Tower, at which a drunken former MP was masturbated by his girlfriend at the back of the room a few feet from Nigel Lawson and other grandees.'[66]

In the final week before the vote, the Tory 'party in the media' made an unusual leap into straightforward campaign spending: Rupert Murdoch's News Group Newspapers, which owned *The Times* and the *Sun*, registered as an official Leave campaign group and spent £96,898 pushing for Brexit.[67]

Odey had a particularly good referendum night: he made £220 million betting that sterling would collapse if, as he hoped, Leave won. He said that the day had broken 'with gold in its mouth'.[68] But in the following months, his flagship fund lost half its value, after he bet on a Brexit-induced recession that didn't materialise.[69]

For an indication of the donors' libertarian bent, some were outraged to have to pay tax on their donations. Edmiston, whose estimated net wealth is in the hundreds of millions, said after being landed with a post-campaign tax bill of £200,000: 'I just feel it is against democracy – if any time in the future someone is asked "would you mind supporting this particular position", the Revenue are going to jump on your back.'[70]

There were also less visible donations to Leave. The funding of online political ads, in particular, is very hard to regulate, or sometimes even trace. The investigative journalist Peter Geoghegan, in his book *Democracy For Sale,* details several other loopholes that allowed political donors to dodge sunshine. For instance, in 2016 donors in Northern Ireland were still allowed to remain anonymous, a hangover from the 'Troubles' era when they risked being murdered. The loophole allowed anyone to give anonymously to pro-Leave entities in Northern Ireland. But there were other ways to hide donations. Look at the strictly Northern-Ireland-only Democratic Unionist Party which made its biggest ever campaign spend on the Brexit referendum. Most of the DUP's funds were invested in a wraparound pro-Leave ad in the *Metro* newspaper in London, which is not in Northern Ireland.

The source of the DUP's money was the party's record donation: £435,000 from something called the Constitutional Research Council. What was that? Geoghegan tried to find out. But whoever was behind the CRC was using another favourite British loophole: the council was a so-called 'unincorporated association'. That meant 'it didn't have to publish an address, list its members or file accounts,' explains Geoghegan. The only physical trace of the CRC's existence was its chairman, Richard Cook, who lived in a semi-detached house in a modest suburb of Glasgow. Cook had booked the *Metro* advert. But he probably wasn't the donor.[71] 'I'm not going to get into the donors,' he said.[72]

The Northern Irish loophole has since been closed. However, unincorporated associations continue to flourish. They are the British equivalent of American 'Super PACs' – the independent political action committees that flood US politics with often untraceable 'dark money'. One notable unincorporated association is the European Research Group.

The hard-Brexit pressure movement within the Tory party raised unknown sums through its dedicated bank account for private donations.[73]

In all, more than £14 million was funnelled to parties through unincorporated associations between 2018 and 2023. The Committee on Standards in Public Life, which advises the government on ethics, called these associations an untransparent 'route for foreign money to influence UK elections'. That hasn't prompted any change.[74]

Back to Vote Leave: even with the help of loopholes, it still broke legal spending limits in the referendum. It spent £449,079.34 more than its statutory maximum of £7 million, ruled the Electoral Commission in 2018.[75] That might sound serious: the official pro-Leave campaign group had broken the laws in a pretty consequential vote. Vote Leave had also declined even to be interviewed about the matter by the Electoral Commission. The Commission had initially refused to investigate the campaign, until a judicial review brought by the barrister Jolyon Maugham's Good Law Project pressured it into doing so.[76] The Commission's reluctance was understandable: any questioning of Vote Leave was a taboo for the Conservatives, because the referendum had become the chief source of their post-Cameron legitimacy.[77]

Though Leave was found guilty, nothing serious was done. The Commission imposed the maximum fine of £20,000, while predicting that Vote Leave would write this off as 'the cost of doing business'. In total, the Commission fined Vote Leave the very manageable sum of £61,000.[78] And with the ruling coming two years after the referendum, hardly anybody even noticed it. The few people making a fuss about the integrity of British elections could be dismissed as 'Remoaners' who needed to 'get over it'.

Vote Leave said the guilty verdict by the non-partisan Commission was 'motivated by a political agenda'.[79] It really ought to have thanked the Commission, which decided that having fined Vote Leave for the one offence, 'it would not be in the public interest to investigate' whether the campaign had also broken the law by illegally coordinating with the DUP. Maugham commented: 'The Electoral Commission seems to think that because Vote Leave has been found guilty of one offence, legally it cannot be found guilty of another one.'[80]

The let-offs for Vote Leave emphasised the vulnerability of British politics to dark money. This is a structural British problem, an inheritance of the Good Chaps era: the country's laws against political corruption are feeble. As the Committee on Standards in Public Life had noted in 2011: 'There have been no successful criminal prosecutions relating to corruption in the giving or receiving of donations to political parties or individual politicians in the last decade.'[81]

English police continue to ignore campaign-finance crimes. They prefer to dump the problem on a toothless watchdog. Police Scotland seem happier to get involved: in 2021 they launched an investigation of the Scottish National Party's donations, and in April 2024 charged the party's former twenty-two-year chief executive, Peter Murrell, husband of former First Minister Nicola Sturgeon, in connection with embezzlement of funds.[82]

Legal authorities were even more aggressive in the US, which has never relied on a Good Chaps theory of government. Around the time that Britain's Electoral Commission slapped its symbolic fines on Vote Leave, Donald Trump's lawyer Michael Cohen was jailed for campaign-finance violations. Trump himself went on trial in spring 2024, charged with having illegally funded his 2016 campaign by paying 'hush money' to the porn star Stormy Daniels. Perhaps Westminster felt a little too superior about American dark money. Rory Stewart was right to express Britain's problem in startlingly American language: 'We need campaign-finance reform.'[83]

★

The Brexit referendum showed donors and politicians the degree of impunity around donations. They would carry those lessons into the future. After

Brexit, the big money returned to the Tory party. The Conservatives' complicated array of donor clubs, tiered by size of donations, gradually dropped the pretence of transparency. Records ceased to be kept of discussions or names of attendees at events. The biggest donors in this era were gathered in the Leaders Group. Of the two hundred or so who attended the group's events from 2013 through 2018, about 97 per cent were male.[84]

First prize for many donors was regular meetings with the prime minister and chancellor. After all, British parties are so centralised that the PM makes all big decisions. Formally, in Britain, the king is the sovereign, and the constitutional mantra is that 'parliament is sovereign', but in practice, the prime minister is sovereign. No wonder, because over time many of the king's traditional powers have been transferred intact to Downing Street.

A British party donor hopes to set the political agenda. If he (and the donor is almost always a he) can persuade the PM or, at worst, a senior minister, of the benefits of his idea, then it's on track to becoming government policy. Ideally, the donor's wish will come to be seen as common sense, and self-evidently good for Britain – for instance, that a certain piece of infrastructure should be built. 'The nature of our system is that if you capture those few minds that are making the big decisions, you've kind of got the ballgame,' says Kate Alexander-Shaw of the London School of Economics.[85]

A British prime minister usually controls both the executive and the legislature. Once the PM resolves to do something, MPs rarely get in the way. They almost always vote the party whip. If they don't, they risk their careers. That makes British political giving much simpler than the US version: American Congresspeople can defy the whip and essentially sell their votes to the highest bidder, so a donor might have to go around squaring dozens of them. British donors can ignore MPs, and usually ignore the Opposition, too. Buy the top of the ruling party and you're done.

Tory donors saw it as their right to tell the PM's circle what they thought. After all, they had paid for it. Some regarded the donors' club as a kind of exclusive informal think-tank. The Conservative donor Stuart Wheeler told the Committee on Standards in Public Life in 2011 that it was 'natural' that donors should influence policy: 'If it is influence in the sense of being able to put their views on what is best for the country and how the country should be run, I do not see any objection to that.'[86]

When rich people buy influence, they typically aren't trying to change the minds of politicians who previously disagreed with them. They fund politicians who already agree with them, and persuade them to push an issue up the agenda. Tory politicians tend to be amenable to donors' advice. Many Tories are cheerleaders for capitalism who are strangely naive about what actual capitalists want from them. They have traditionally been in awe of buccaneering businessmen, from Lord Hanson and Jimmy Goldsmith to Crispin Odey. If a donor wants a change to economic policy, well, maybe it's an altruistic suggestion that would benefit the nation.

The more dinners that Tory ministers eat with donors, the more they come to see the world from the donors' point of view: such a generous chap, and such a travesty that those unimaginative blockers at HMRC tried to hit him with that punitive tax bill.

Head-spinningly, some ministers go back and forth between donors and poor constituents. Willetts says that when he was a minister, 'You would literally on Thursday be at dinner with millionaires, some of them would write a cheque for £50,000, and then on Friday in your constituency a woman would come in asking how she could feed her children over the weekend because her benefits had run out.' Politicians are impacted by both kinds of encounters. But typically, the constituent has a problem (usually something intractable involving government bureaucracy) whereas the donor has an opinion.

Better yet, donors and Tory politicians have a natural affinity: they are mostly privately educated right-wing men. Any quid pro quo between them rarely needs to be made explicit. Each side understands the other. And their agreements seldom break any rules, because British government doesn't have many written rules. This is a very British form of corruption, disguised as friendship.

During a donor's meeting, there'd often be a question in the politician's mind: what's my next career move? Senior politicians are almost by definition ambitious people. They have been planning their careers since kindergarten. Even while in cabinet they're looking ahead, which means that every meeting with a rich person is a semiconscious job interview. No sitting minister needs to be so gauche as to take a donor's bribe. Instead, you can just phone the chap after you leave politics.

These days, after all, political careers can end in an instant. Politicians have seen countless colleagues turfed out of Westminster before the age of fifty. As I write this, many Conservative ministers expect to be out of a job within weeks. There you might be, at the lowest moment in your professional life, unemployed but with school fees still to pay. All your career you've earned less than certain chums from university. Now, post-politics, you intend to cash in. Given your profession's collapsing status, you'll be in little demand from PLCs, who are no longer proud to put a politician on the board. Who to turn to? Well, why not the donors with whom you spent so many agreeable evenings? Perhaps you could find work introducing them to your old friends who are still in politics.

*

Tories spent donors' money less on direct campaigning than on long-term investments. These were particularly necessary after Theresa May's debacle in the 2017 election, when, faced with the surmountable challenge of Jeremy Corbyn, she contrived to lose the Conservative majority. The Tories' data and analytics had failed in the campaign: canvassers repeatedly showed up at homes that they believed contained potential supporters, only to be shouted at by people who loathed Tories. Afterwards, the party invested to improve data and analytics, built up the marketing and membership sections at party headquarters, and doubled staff in Conservative Research Department.[87]

But May never won the donors' trust. That was a dangerous vulnerability. Because PMs are their parties' ultimate fundraisers, they are in personal jeopardy if the donors turn against them – if, in modern Westminster jargon, they 'lose the money'. That's what happened almost simultaneously to May and Corbyn. Her push for a moderate Brexit, in which the UK would stay aligned with European regulations, alienated the Tories' mostly hard-Brexit donors.[88]

Her end was hastened in 2019 when some donors defected to Nigel Farage's Brexit Party, which was calling for a hard Brexit or No Deal.[89] Christopher Harborne, a British entrepreneur living in Thailand, where he is also known as Chakrit Sakunkrit, gave the Brexit Party £9.7 million – the largest donation to any British party that year.[90] When Harborne arrived in party headquarters, he bought a fridge and a coffee machine, but above all, he funded rallies and campaigning. The Brexit Party won twenty-nine seats in the European Parliament in May 2019, briefly becoming the body's largest single party.[91]

For all Harborne's political power, he remains almost unknown to British voters. But the short-lived Brexit Party had a lasting impact: May fell and was replaced by Johnson, who promised a hard Brexit. Anthony Bamford[92] was one of the delighted Tory donors. In 2019, reports the *Guardian*, 'Johnson drove a JCB digger through a wall of polystyrene bricks emblazoned with the words "Get Brexit done"'.[93]

*

When Johnson became prime minister, he opened the doors to donors like no party leader before him. The Conservatives no longer even pretended to want to curb money in politics. Their insouciance made sense: four straight election victories had taught them that voters didn't punish them for taking millions from rich people (or, indeed, for anything else). As Peter Geoghegan asks, when was the last mass demonstration against money in politics?[94]

Johnson immediately appointed his suave friend and fellow Old Etonian, Ben Elliot, as the Conservatives' co-chair and de facto chief fundraiser. Elliot carried the party to new heights of donor-friendliness. His story is central to any account of money in British politics. In telling it, I am leaning largely on investigative reporting by my *Financial Times* colleagues, especially George Parker, Sebastian Payne, Tom Burgis, Kadhim Shubber, Jim Pickard and Jasmine Cameron-Chileshe.

But Elliot's origins were most fully reported by the *Tatler*, house journal of the British upper class. The magazine writes[95] that he was raised in 'a Grade II-listed Queen Anne house' in Dorset with swimming pool and tennis court. His grandfathers sound like archetypal Good Chaps. The one, Sir William Elliot, was 'air officer commanding-in-chief at RAF Fighter Command (he once crashed behind enemy lines and staged a gutsy escape)'. The other, Major Bruce Shand, won two Military Crosses. (Elliot wore Shand's 1970s Rolex.) Shand's daughter, Elliot's aunt, is Queen Camilla.

At Eton, Elliot interviewed Margaret Thatcher for the school magazine. Like many Etonians, he later moved in an old-school milieu in London. 'He was there when Prince William first had a drink,' reports *Tatler*. Elliot dated beautiful posh women. He consorted with the billionaire heir Zac Goldsmith and Johnson at Aspinalls, a private gaming club in Mayfair with a high Old-Etonian quotient.

Elliot co-founded a concierge company for the super rich called Quintessentially, which promised its clients 'anything you want, anytime you want it, anywhere you want it'.[96] Its reported feats included closing Sydney Harbour Bridge for a marriage proposal, organising lunch on an iceberg,[97] and, reports the *FT*, 'shipping a dozen albino peacocks to a party for Jennifer Lopez' as well as 'airlifting elm tea bags to Madonna'. Elliot called himself 'a willing slave to the stars'.[98] He often charmed them at Robin Birley's club, 5 Hertford Street.[99]

In 2013 Quintessentially built the website of an international escort agency named Le Besoin, which offered 'high class models' to 'high-profile gentlemen' in cities including London, New York and Moscow. The site was registered to Quintessentially's office at London's Portland Place. Quintessentially said later it had 'created a website for a client launching a dating service', and had no further involvement 'after completion of the website and branding project'.[100]

Quintessentially ran offices in sixty cities, employing fifty staff in Russia. It also had a dedicated Russia team based in London.[101] Its Russian-language site, featuring the slogan, 'Access the inaccessible. Achieve the impossible', was still up the day Russian troops invaded Ukraine in 2022.[102]

After the Brexit referendum, Quintessentially won a contract (reportedly worth £1.4 million) with the Department of International Trade to 'attract foreign direct investment to the UK by focusing on high-net-worth individual investors'. The company was to 'bring subject matter expertise and best practice from the luxury concierge industry into the programme'.[103] Despite this frenzy of activity, Quintessentially was losing money even before the pandemic hit.[104]

The tireless Elliot also cofounded the lobbying and PR firm Hawthorn Advisers, whose clients, reported the *FT*, 'included a now-banned Chinese tech giant' and 'the chairman of a Russian oligarch's aluminium business'.[105]

Elliot had long dabbled in Conservative politics. He looked into becoming an MP, and served as campaign treasurer for Zac Goldsmith's run for mayor of London in 2016; he and Goldsmith had known each other since they were seven. Goldsmith had previously ruled out a mayoral run, saying, 'I think people have had quite enough of white male Etonians.'[106] He should have stuck with his instinct: his campaign was criticised as islamophobic, and ended in disaster.

Elliot's political ambitions survived the wreckage.

Johnson, who craved money but hated asking for it, saw he could leave all that to his friend. Elliot would charm donors with a mockney working-class accent, and later get tough to seal the deal: 'You owe us the money.'

In essence, he transferred Quintessentially's model of cash-for-access to British politics. The more a Tory donor paid, the better their access. The Conservatives had long been chasing rich people, but ahead of the general election of 2019, Elliot turned the dial up to eleven. The Leaders Group had been the party's top-tier donors' club, with members expected to cough up at least £50,000, but Elliot considered it too cheap. He installed a level above it: the invitation-only Advisory Board. Its existence was not documented and its members were not named,[107] but they were granted monthly meetings with either Johnson or his chancellor, Rishi Sunak.[108]

Tory donors and Quintessentially clients overlapped. The international telecoms deal-maker Mohamed Amersi, who will pop up again in Chapter Five, had joined Quintessentially's 'Global Elite' tier, at a cost of £15,000 a year. In 2013 Elliot arranged for his uncle, Prince Charles, to dine with Amersi and his younger Russian-born partner Nadezhda Rodicheva. Amersi says Quintessentially's Global Elite members received introductions to other royals too.[109] A spokesman for Quintessentially said the meetings were to raise funds for charity.

Amersi told the *FT* that Elliot 'started seeking donations from me and Nadia for the Conservative Party even before he became chair'. Inconveniently, Amersi was initially registered as a 'non-dom', meaning non-domiciled in Britain, a status that has tax advantages. He has a townhouse in Mayfair, five minutes' walk from 5 Hertford Street, but his main base was Dubai.[110] Since he wasn't on the British electoral roll, he couldn't legally donate to a party. That was soon fixed. On 28 April 2017, reports Tom Burgis in his book *Cuckooland*, Amersi 'emails a Conservative Party fundraiser, copying in Ben Elliot: "Can I now send the funds in my name or should Nadia do it?"' The answer: Nadia should, because Amersi wouldn't make the electoral roll until June 1.[111]

The pretence was that the donation came from Nadia, not from the ineligible Amersi. Yet the Tories' email to arrange payment began, according to Burgis: 'Dear Mr Amersi. Thank you so much for the extremely generous donation of £200k from Nadia. Please find below our bank details for the transfer.' Amersi's lawyers sent Burgis bank documents indicating that it was Nadia Rodicheva who made the payment.[112]

After May's ousting in 2019, Amersi spread his bets among the plausible leadership contenders: £10,000 each for Johnson, Michael Gove and Jeremy Hunt.[113] His and Nadia's joint donations of about £750,000 from 2017 through 2021 were only enough to buy him membership of the Leaders Group, not of the Advisory Board. That club, said Amersi, was 'like the very elite Quintessentially clients' membership: one needs to cough up £250,000 per annum or be a friend of Ben'.[114]

Elliot seemed to do a better job for the Tories than he had for Quintessentially. In the year to the 2019 election, the party raised a record £37.4 million in 'large' donations, enough to keep going for years to come. When a triumphant Johnson and his partner Carrie Symonds arrived at Conservative Campaign Headquarters on election night, the first person they hugged was Elliot.[115]

Straight after the election, the buccaneering donors quickly got their way on the UK's biggest immediate policy decision: Johnson delivered a hard Brexit. That choice would shape the UK for decades.

But donors have lost some battles on other issues. Only intermittently does the Tory party act as the executive wing of the buccaneering super rich. Just as voters often feel taken in by the Conservatives, so do donors. Part of Elliot's skill was to persuade rich people to pay fortunes for an uncertain return. Yes, they got to meet the PM, but lots of other people met the PM for free.

Donors are just one of the rival factions fighting for control of the party. Any Tory leader will listen to them, but will listen even harder to the electorate. Take the donors' battles against high taxes and Covid lockdowns. At a gathering at a Kensington townhouse in June 2021, hosted by the banker Rishi Khosla, donors chastised Johnson about 'state intervention'. He tried to pacify them by promising to go ahead with 'Freedom Day' – the high-risk lifting of most of England's Covid-19 restrictions scheduled for 19 July.[116] The donors got their Freedom Day, but, too often for their liking, they lost their tug-of-war with the government's scientific advisers.

Johnson also had to balance donors' pleas for tax cuts with the need to fund the public services that ordinary voters relied on. The donors suffered their biggest defeat on taxes. By 2024, the Tories had raised Britain's overall taxation to the highest percentage of gross domestic product in over seventy years.[117]

Property developers had particular reason to feel betrayed by Johnson. They are always generous givers to the ruling party, presumably because it decides what they can build, and how. They became even more generous under Johnson: from 2019 through 2021 their giving jumped to nearly £18 million, accounting for a quarter of all Conservative donations.[118]

In 2020, under the slogan 'build, build, build', Johnson promised to lift many of the planning and environmental restrictions that they loathed. It was to be the biggest transformation of the planning system since 1947. Donors loved it. But when traditional Tory NIMBY homeowners failed to embrace 'build build build', and the Conservatives lost the Chesham and Amersham by-election in 2021, the plans were quietly jettisoned.[119]

Still, even if a property developer couldn't have laws changed, he might get something for his money. In 2019, at a Conservative fundraising dinner at the Savoy Hotel arranged by Elliot, where tickets cost more than £900, the billionaire property developer, former porn baron, *Daily Express* owner, and occasional Tory donor Richard Desmond was lucky enough to be seated next to housing secretary Robert Jenrick. Better yet, because it was a political event, there were no pesky civil servants surrounding the minister taking notes and interrupting. Desmond wanted to build 1,500 homes on London's Isle of Dogs, in Tower Hamlets council. Unfortunately, people like London's mayor, Sadiq Khan, were blocking the scheme because, Desmond explained, they were 'just trying to stop Britain being great'.

Desmond took out his phone and showed Jenrick a glitzy video of the planned development. Afterwards he repeatedly texted Jenrick, urging him to give the go-ahead before Tower Hamlets' new tax on big developments took effect: 'We appreciate the speed as we don't want to give Marxists loads of doe [sic] for nothing.'[120]

It was classic British politics: a minister is poorly informed about his subject area (Jenrick had only been in the job for four months) and doesn't understand the complicated processes of his own department, so he is swayed by a persuasive donor who sidesteps the civil servants.

Jenrick okayed Desmond's scheme, against advice from Tower Hamlets council, one day before the new tax went into force. That saved Desmond £40 million. Jenrick also waived rules on affordable housing, which, the property consultancy BNP Paribas Real Estate calculated later, saved Desmond another £106 million. A fortnight after Jenrick's decision, Desmond donated £12,000 to the Tories. Cheap at twice the price – indeed, at several hundred times the price. At the same Savoy dinner, incidentally, Mohamed Amersi paid £100,000 at auction for breakfast with Johnson.[121]

The Jenrick–Desmond affair raises the question posed in the title of a famous academic paper on American campaign contributions: 'Why Is There So Little Money in Politics?'[122] Given the size of the government's economic impact, the cost of political influence is remarkably low – especially in the UK, the deep-discount version of American politics.

In the event, Desmond's flutter on Jenrick failed to pay off. Tower Hamlets council, another member of the stop-Britain-being-great brigade, appealed Jenrick's decision. Jenrick then accepted that his call had been 'unlawful' because it had created the 'appearance of bias'.[123] The rule of law still often works in Britain. In a sense, Jenrick got unlucky: usually, by the time an act of political favouritism turns sour, years have passed and the politician in question has moved on or been forgotten. The Desmond–Jenrick story was a rare visualisation of how a lot of normally unseen business gets done in London.

Other donors seek other rewards. Maybe they want to chair the BBC, or join the board of a regulatory watchdog, or become a non-executive director (NED) in a ministry that they're interested in. Take the venture capitalist Lord John Nash, a second-tier Tory donor. He invested in academy schools, became a NED in the education department, was made a peer by David Cameron and then became schools minister.

In 2020 Johnson appointed Nash the government's 'Lead NED', which meant he would have a central role in recruiting new NEDs.[124] Few citizens even know that this powerful role exists. Nash also became 'Cabinet Office NED'. He held these posts until 2022. NEDs advise government departments, among other things, on procurement – buying goods and services from companies. Meanwhile, NEDs acquire commercially sensitive inside information on important bits of government.

While Nash held senior government posts, he was simultaneously earning fortunes from government contracts. Companies in which he had a financial interest received more than £3.8 billion from government from 2016 through early 2024, reported the *New Statesman*. Nash-linked companies 'have been paid more than 180,000 times by government departments, local authorities, NHS trusts, police services and a wide range of other public bodies,' wrote the magazine. One company, the IT group Softcat, in which Nash owned a stake worth over £88 million, had 'billed the public sector for £2.97 billion across more than 47,000 invoices since 2016'.

There is no suggestion of wrongdoing by Nash or the companies. But he does seem to have a conflict of interest. Margaret Hodge, the Labour MP, commented that for a peer and former minister to make millions in this way 'simply adds to the public's view that everybody in politics is only in it for themselves'.[125]

These kinds of jobs for donors have multiplied since the Cameron era. The pre-2010 way to fill public-sector roles had been for a panel, with some nudging from the minister, to draw up a shortlist of qualified Good Chaps. The minister then got to pick the winner. But the post-Brexit Conservatives viewed old-style Good Chaps as a conspiracy of ghastly unelected Islington Remoaners.

Tory Brexiters intended to build a new establishment. They tried to install more of their own sympathisers on appointment panels, with the aim of appointing sympathisers to top jobs. More and more, it was the minister and their special advisers who drew up the list of candidates for public-sector roles. It was especially handy if you could install a friend on the board of a watchdog that had grown any teeth.

Donors always needed to be kept happy, and some of them craved these roles. Donors had access to a biweekly appointment list from Number Ten. The PM's appointments unit helped them apply for posts.[126]

Partisan appointments probably peaked under Johnson. His government even tried to block the classicist Mary Beard from becoming a trustee of the British Museum, because she opposed Brexit.[127] Seemingly non-strategic roles at cultural institutions increasingly went to donors.[128] In what sounds like a joke about modern Britain, donors made up a big chunk of the board of the Social Mobility Commission.[129]

There remains a check on hyper-partisanship: an 'advisory assessment panel' can decide whether the candidates put forward by ministers are 'appointable'. But these panels tend to block only truly outrageous nominees – Paul Dacre, long-time hyper-partisan editor of the *Daily Mail*, didn't get to run the media regulator Ofcom – while passing the marginally outrageous.[130] After all, Johnson's Tories were elected, the panels weren't, and Tory-supporting tabloids were scary.

★

During the long slow death of Johnson's premiership, the Conservatives held their annual Summer Ball fundraiser at the Victoria and Albert Museum. The big prize at the traditional auction, writes Tim Bale, even more sought-after than the African safari and the shooting weekend, was 'dinner with Johnson, May, and Cameron (together in the same room apparently), which reportedly went for around £120,000.'[131] The implicit message from the winning bidder to the three prime ministers was, 'I own you.'

In July 2022, Johnson and his new wife Carrie held their wedding party at the Bamfords' Cotswold estate. Meanwhile, Liz Truss, Sunak and their battalions of donors were squaring up for the campaign to replace Johnson. She held her 'Fizz with Liz' meetings with backbenchers at 5 Hertford Street.[132] Her meetings with donors were branded 'Biz with Liz'.[133] Sunak, with his background in finance, outraised her, pulling in £458,570 in donations as well as the use of office space and a private jet.[134] Yet the party's remaining 172,000 members, some of them probably leftovers from the 1950s' membership heyday, went for Truss.

Hours after her victory, Ben Elliot resigned as

Conservative co-chair. Darren Mott, the party's chief executive, said in tribute: 'Without his incredible efforts, the 2019 landslide would not have been possible.'[135] During Johnson's farewell speech outside Number Ten, there, standing behind him, was Elliot.[136]

Truss's premiership is fondly remembered by at least one Tory donor. During her campaign, the hedge-funder Crispin Odey had lunch at his home with his former employee Kwasi Kwarteng, Truss's future chancellor. Odey said later: 'We have never discussed anything but the usual gossip of politics.' Yet he somehow seems to have got wind of Truss and Kwarteng's economic plans. When their budget of unfunded tax cuts for the rich sank British assets, Odey made a fortune betting on the pound's collapse.[137]

In June 2023, the *Financial Times* and *Tortoise Media* revealed the long list of allegations of sexual assault against Odey. He was then expelled from his own hedge fund, Odey Asset Management. Nonetheless, two months later, Reform UK, the latest incarnation of Farage's Brexit Party, accepted his donation of £10,000.[138] As John Bowers notes, you have to pass a 'fit and proper person test' to own a British football club, but not to donate to a political party.[139]

Reform initially wrongly reported that the £10,000 gift came from an industry think tank. When the donor's identity emerged later, the party's leader

Richard Tice said the incorrect logging had been 'a simple clerical error'. Asked whether he had known about the *FT*'s allegations when taking Odey's money, Tice dismissed the *FT* as 'a trendy lefty newspaper'.[140]

Tice's supposedly working-class Reform party relied overwhelmingly on 'donors linked to climate science denial and fossil fuel investments', reported the green activist group DeSmog.[141] Reform's biggest funders were Harborne, who owns an aviation fuel supplier and trades private jets,[142] and Jeremy Hosking, a major investor in fossil fuels.[143] It must have hurt the Conservatives to see their former moneymen fund a rival party.

When Sunak became prime minister, the former 'hedgie' revived the bruised confidence of many donors. Heading for the most expensive general election in British history, even as the Tory party lagged Labour by twenty points in the polls, it was winning five to one on donations. In the third quarter of 2023, Labour pulled in its biggest quarterly haul in the party's history: £3.1 million, including donations from unions. The Conservatives scored £15.4 million.[144]

Just in case Britain's rules on political donations weren't lax enough, Sunak's government raised the spending limits on campaigns for the first time since 2000, from £19.5 million per party to £35 million. He seems to have presumed that only the Conservatives would have that much to spend. The threshold at which donations had to be declared jumped from £7,500 to £11,180. True, the rises were in line with inflation. Still, you might have thought there were democratic reasons to curb money in politics, not expand it. Punishments for rule-breaches remained piffling. In April 2024, the Electoral Commission identified fourteen offences by the Conservatives involving 'donations inaccurately reported, and donations and loans reported late'. The total fine was £1,500.[145]

Like in a doping-fuelled Olympic sport, records for donations were broken all the time. Mohamed Mansour's gift of £5 million in 2023 was the highest in the Tories' history, but months later, John Sainsbury's will bequeathed £10 million to the Conservative Party Foundation, which funds bursaries for parliamentary candidates.[146]

Frank Hester almost immediately equalled Sainsbury's record, giving £10 million directly to the Tory party in the year through early 2024.[147] Hester had trained as a priest before becoming an entrepreneur in healthcare technology. The *Guardian* newspaper revealed that at a meeting of his company, the Phoenix Partnership, in 2019, he had said of an executive at another organisation:

> She's the shittest person. Honestly I try not to be sexist but when I meet somebody like [her],

I just ... It's like trying not to be racist but you see [Labour MP] Diane Abbott on the TV, and you're just like I hate, you just want to hate all black women because she's there, and I don't hate all black women at all, but I think she should be shot.

[The executive] and Diane Abbott need to be shot ... If we can get [the executive] being unprofessional we can get her sacked. It's not as good as her dying. It would be much better if she died.[148]

When the remarks sparked outrage, the Conservatives protected Hester. As well they might: *Tortoise Media* revealed that the party was 'sitting on' yet another £5 million gift from him.[149] In all, that would make Hester easily the most generous donor in British political history.

Still, perhaps we oughtn't worry about his outsized influence. Lord Marland, former Tory party treasurer and donor, explained that Hester 'does a lot of business in Jamaica, he does business in Malaysia, in Bangladesh and places like that so he's not a racist'.[150] Weeks after the scandal broke, the pressure on the Tories to return Hester's money had evaporated. The story moved on. The British public has become unshockable.

4

RUSSIAN PIONEERS

The West has degraded so much that I don't see any
difference in these political systems any longer. If I
had to choose between Theresa May, Corbyn or Putin,
I would choose Putin. He is the best politician.

Alexander Lebedev, the former KGB agent who bought
the *Evening Standard* and *Independent* newspapers, 2019[1]

It's problematic enough when rich people essentially
buy shares in the British ruling party. It's even more
problematic when some of those people have ties
to dangerous and corrupt autocracies such as Russia. The Conservatives, the nativist party of regional
England, are now funded by a London-based international elite.

I should say in advance that the problem isn't that
donors have a mix of foreign and British allegiances.
I have a mix of foreign and British allegiances myself.
I was born in Uganda to South African parents, spent
most of my school years in the Netherlands, and now
live in Paris. The problem is when people get rich

through political connections in foreign autocracies, then put money into British politics, while in many cases retaining allegiances to those autocracies. How did rich Russians pioneer foreign investment into Westminster?

Corruption comes home

In the days when the UK was a global power, corruption usually happened the other way around: Britons bribed foreigners. This was so routine into the 1990s that British companies sometimes hired investigators to recover bribes if foreign recipients didn't deliver the agreed quid pro quo.[2]

The biggest case of British bribery surrounded the secretive Al Yamamah arms deal, originally negotiated by Thatcher in 1985, to supply British weapons to Saudi Arabia. Wafic Saïd, the Syrian-Saudi-Canadian businessman who helped broker Al Yamamah, was a major funder of the Conservatives until the PPERA Act of 2000 barred foreign donors. His son Khaled donated to Rory Stewart's campaign to become Tory leader.[3] Wafic's British wife Rosemary (who wasn't involved in Al Yamamah) was still giving to the Tories in 2021.[4]

The original Al Yamamah agreement spawned further arms deals worth tens of billions over subsequent decades. My newspaper, the *FT*, called Al

Yamamah 'the biggest sale of anything British to anyone ever'.[5] But the sale was stained from the start: the British arms maker BAE Systems and its predecessor were accused of bribing Saudi royals and others with sums that may have run into billions.

Jonathan Aitken, minister for defence procurement under John Major, benefited personally from some Saudi bribes. When his libel case against media that reported this collapsed in 1997, the *Guardian* ran the delicious front-page headline, 'He lied and lied and lied.'[6] Aitken was jailed for perjury.

The Serious Fraud Office later launched a criminal inquiry into Al Yamamah, but Tony Blair's government blocked it in 2006, saying that continuing the inquiry would endanger British lives. The Saudis had threatened to stop cooperating on intelligence in the 'war on terror'. The Ministry of Defence authorised secret quarterly payments from BAE to Saudi Prince Bandar bin Sultan, totalling over £1 billion in all, until at least 2007.[7] In 2010 BAE struck a plea bargain over Al Yamamah, and paid fines totalling nearly $450 million.[8]

But by then the traffic in dubious payments had started to reverse direction. Corruption was coming home to Britain. Many of the ex-Soviets who grabbed the oil, gas and minerals of the collapsing USSR brought the proceeds to London. It became their back office, playground and money launderette. Then, after the financial crisis of 2008, the UK's need for foreign money became acute. The government issued thousands of 'Tier 1 investor' or so-called 'golden' visas. Almost any foreigner who committed to investing £1 million (increased to £2 million in 2014) could get residency, and a fast-track to British citizenship, with nobody showing much interest in how they had acquired the money. About 2,600 Russians received British golden visas from 2008 through 2021.[9] The Chinese got even more. 'Londongrad' welcomed kleptocrats. From the mighty Treasury downwards, under both New Labour and the Tories, there was a British consensus in favour of an 'open economy'.

In the years before Putin annexed Crimea in 2014, hardly anyone in the British state perceived a threat from Russia. The domestic intelligence service MI5 was focused on Islamic terrorism. In 2008/2009 it devoted just 3 per cent of its efforts to countering 'Hostile State Activity', which included China, Iran and other states beside Russia.[10]

Even the annexation of Crimea hardly dented Londongrad. Russians accused of corruption or links to the Kremlin bought £1.5 billion worth of British property between 2016 and early 2022, reported Transparency International UK. The NGO added that this estimate was 'the tip of the iceberg' since many Russians bought homes through shell companies.[11] 'There is, in effect, a "For Sale" sign hanging over the United Kingdom,' wrote the MP Margaret Hodge.[12] One effect of the incoming wealth was to make Tory politicians, in particular, feel even poorer than they already did. Their schoolfriends were multi-millionaires, but some of London's new foreigners were billionaires.

The high-end international influx went well beyond Russians. To get a sense of the rich variety of foreigners that a British politician could meet, look at the social life of Labour's Peter Mandelson. He developed a relationship with the infamous American paedophile financier Jeffrey Epstein, stayed off the coast of Corfu on the yacht of Russian oligarch Oleg Deripaska (since sanctioned by western countries), and on another Corfu holiday, this time as a guest of Nat Rothschild's family, met a son of Libya's then leader Colonel Gaddafi.[13]

London's new rich came from everywhere. Kazakhstan alone provided 206 applicants for golden visas. 'As Kazakhstan is a country where just 162 people own 55 per cent of the wealth,' noted a Chatham House report, 'this suggests that the UK may have granted residency to a significant proportion of that country's kleptocratic elite.' In 2020, the owners of a 'super apartment' in Chelsea worth £40 million were revealed to be the daughter and grandson of Nursultan Nazarbayev, Kazakhstan's president from 1991 until 2019.[14]

Even British royals could be reverse-colonised. In 2007 Nazarbayev's billionaire son-in-law Timor Kulibayev bought Prince Andrew's long-unsold mansion Sunninghill Park for £15 million. That was £3 million above the asking price, despite there being no rival bids. 'I can't believe all the fuss about this stupid house!' Kulibayev's former partner, the Kazakh businesswoman Goga Ashkenazi, told me. 'I introduced them, so what? I'm not a real estate agent. All the speculation about the price – I think they just didn't want to barter with a royal.'[15]

Many subsequent newcomers also sprinkled money on British royals or their causes. It was amusing, status-enhancing, and a conversation starter at social events. It was nice for the royals, too. Between 2011 and 2015, Prince Charles received three perfectly legal donations totalling €3 million in cash for his charities from Qatar's former prime minister Sheikh Hamad bin Jassim. 'HBJ', as he is known, handed over one gift in a small suitcase, another in a holdall, and a third in carrier bags from Fortnum & Mason.[16]

Prince Michael of Kent was more business-minded than his cousin. In 2021 Michael and his associate the Marquess of Reading were filmed telling undercover reporters posing as Korean businesspeople that Michael could help introduce them to contacts in the Kremlin.[17]

The Russians wanted to have fun in London too. They liked it that in Knightsbridge they didn't haven't to worry much about being jailed or gunned down in a restaurant after falling out with the local autocrat. They bought the Barbour jacket, the Aston Martin and the stately home, starting the time-honoured journey from robber baron to gentleman. Their British public relations advisers, armed with public-school accents and cufflinks, got them invited to gallery openings, charity galas and even shooting weekends at the homes of actual (if hard-up) dukes. The newcomers' kids were channelled into the ruling caste's schools. In 2016, when Putin hadn't yet met Britain's new prime minister Theresa May, he received eleven boys from Eton for a friendly discussion of world affairs.[18]

Many Russian donations to the Tories had an element of social climbing. The newcomers yearned to meet posh Britons. They hadn't been to school or Oxford with them, but they discovered they could get invited to high-Tory fundraising dinners in London clubs by donating to the toffs' ancestral political party. It wasn't so different from giving to a royal charity, or paying to put your name on a plaque at Oxford or Cambridge. At Conservative events you might spot a nervous foreign wife, in a new dress and wearing too much jewellery, praying that a British aristo with his English-rose debutante would stop and say hello.

In the dream scenario, the Russians would end up inviting them to stay in their Cotswolds stately home.

The British ruling caste tries to look exclusive but is always open to rich, talented or beautiful newcomers, even if it salvages some self-esteem by sniggering at their accents and jewellery. Posh Britons have been looking down on garish upstarts since the late Victorian era when they first had to replenish the coffers by marrying rich Americans. (Lady Randolph Churchill, Winston's mother, was born in Brooklyn as Jenny Jerome.) However, the garish Russians also looked down on posh Britons, perhaps with more reason. After all, the Britons had let them in unquestioned.

The newcomers weren't in London just to play. They had learned back home the need to buy political protection in case they ran into any bother with media, courts or security services. Many newcomers aimed to keep their old connections with the Kremlin, while adding new ones in Westminster. There you were, a newbie in London, without a network, and you realised: you could build it from the prime minister on down. The old pros steamrollered the British dilettantes.

Beautifully, for those Russians who still had one foot in Moscow, their donations to the Tories enhanced their standing with Putin. They could trade their access to British power for favours from the Kremlin, because the Kremlin cared about British power. Some Russians, when visiting Moscow, exaggerated their influence in London. Others may have ended up with more influence in London than in Putin's Moscow.

The flood of foreign money into politics in the 2010s happened in many countries.[19] Several trends in globalisation encouraged it: ever more major powers (notably China, Russia and Qatar) sought influence abroad; ever more national economies were permeable to foreign money; and ever more billionaires could afford to buy foreign political parties.

US politicians had grown so pricey that many American donors saw better returns on investment in smaller economies. For instance, a few American families typically provided over 90 per cent of the funding for the Israeli prime minister Binyamin Netanyahu's primary campaigns. Dutch far-right leader Geert Wilders raised funds from anti-Islamic American groups.

And Russia financed many foreign political systems. Most notably, the First Czech–Russia bank lent the far-right French Front National €9.4m in 2014, around the time that the Front's leader, Marine Le Pen, endorsed Russia's annexation of Crimea. Leaked text messages between Russian officials suggested that the loan's approval was the Kremlin's way to say thank you.[20]

China helped out some African ruling parties.

Qatar funded Islamist movements during the Arab Spring (mostly betting on losing horses). Allies of Malaysian prime minister Najib Razak explained that the mysterious $681 million discovered in his personal bank account was a political donation from the Saudi royal family. Years later, the US Democratic Senator Bob Menendez went on trial charged with having taken bribes to act as an agent of Egypt while he was chair of the Senate Foreign Relations Committee. He pleaded not guilty.

National political systems everywhere were malfunctioning in an unregulated globalised world. Yet few places were as open to foreign money as London.

'People here are very inexpensive to corrupt,' Bill Browder, an American investor in Russia turned anti-corruption activist, told the journalist Gavin Esler. 'It's ridiculous how cheap the whole system is. For £50,000 or £75,000 people will do the most unbelievable things ... I don't know what it is about this country. Maybe [it's] this weird colonial culture where everyone thinks everything is savage everywhere else, and we're all good here.' Browder said that for a Russian oligarch, £75,000 was like a tip for a concierge.[21]

London's libel lawyers, accountants, estate agents, public-relations advisers, sex workers, dog-walkers, footballers, bodyguards and private-school headteachers were all taking dodgy foreign money.

London's politicians were just an underpaid bit of the system. They might, understandably, have thought: 'Everyone does it.'

The moment Russians became British citizens, they were allowed to give to political parties. From about 2012 through 2022, they were the foreign nationality that topped the list of British political donations. Naturally, they gave to the ruling party rather than the powerless Opposition.

The Tories were delighted. It was as if extraterrestrials had stepped out of a spaceship on Parliament Square and inexplicably begun handing them money. The Russian you met over whiskies in 5 Hertford Street was charming. Of course he wasn't working for the Kremlin! Don't go all Le Carré on me. And if you did make the effort to perform the most basic due diligence on where his money came from, well that might get in the way of taking it. Better not to know. If the source of a particular donation was unmissably embarrassing even to the wilfully blind, then any halfway competent party treasurer could time its declaration for a period when nobody was paying much attention – weeks after a general election, say.

In any case, most British politicians had British political obsessions and knew little about faraway countries. Newly minted MPs and ministers didn't receive briefings explaining to them that they had just become walking targets for bad actors. Nothing had gone horribly wrong in Britain for over three hundred years – no invasions, revolutions, famines, or civil wars – and so British politicians had a tendency to feel relaxed.

Russian-born British citizens penetrated to the heart of the Conservative Party. Take Lubov Chernukhin, whose husband Vladimir had become Russian deputy finance minister under Putin aged just thirty-two. Later, a presidential decree appointed him chairman of Russia's state development bank.[22] Vladimir made tens of millions of dollars while a state employee, then fell out with Putin in 2004 and moved to the UK.[23] The Chernukhins (through a company registered in the British Virgin Islands) paid the Crown Estates £18 million for 1 Cambridge Gate, a stuccoed marvel facing Regents Park.[24]

Lubov began donating to the Tories in 2012. She became a fixture at the Conservative Black and White fundraising balls.[25] In 2014, at an auction at the Conservative summer party at Fulham's Hurlingham Club, she paid £160,000 to play tennis with David Cameron and Boris Johnson.[26] In 2019 she paid £135,000 to attend a ladies' night dinner attended by the prime minister Theresa May and Liz Truss.[27] In 2020, after Johnson became PM, Chernukhin bought more tennis with him.[28] By 2023, she had given the party more than £2.4 million,[29] becoming one of its top ten donors, and its biggest female donor (admittedly in a slim field). The *FT* identified her as a member of the party's 'Advisory Board', which had monthly meetings with Johnson or Sunak when they were prime minister and chancellor.[30]

Lubov Chernukhin's money cannot be disentangled from the Russian regime. A Chatham House report says: 'An October 2021 Pandora Papers investigation claimed that her wealth flows through Vladimir's secretive offshore structures which "raises the question over the extent to which it is Vladimir, not Lubov, who may be the ultimate source of some of the cash flowing into the Conservative Party".'[31] She confirmed in a court case in 2018 that her husband maintained 'excellent' relationships with 'prominent members of the Russian establishment'.[32]

This seems to have been true. In 2016 Vladimir received $8 million from an offshore company linked with Suleyman Kerimov, a Russian oligarch and government official. By 2022, Kerimov had been sanctioned by Australia, Canada, the EU, Japan, New Zealand, Switzerland, the US and UK.[33] The EU called him 'a member of the inner circle of oligarchs' close to Putin.[34]

The Chatham House report notes:

Lawyers representing the Chernukhins declined to say whether Vladimir Chernukhin had received this $8 million [from Kerimov], but stated that

Lubov Chernukhina had never received money derived from Kerimov or any company related to him. They added that Lubov's donations to the Conservative Party had never been 'tainted by Kremlin or any other influence' and had been declared in accordance with Electoral Commission rules.[35]

The BBC saw a document dated 2006, signed by Chernukhin under her maiden name of Lubov Gulobeva, which listed her as a director of an offshore company secretly owned by Kerimov. Asked about this, her lawyers said she 'does not recall consenting in writing' to being a director. They suggested that the documents were 'forgeries and/or may have been manipulated'.[36] (Lubov Chernukhin condemned 'Russian military aggression in Ukraine' after the 2022 invasion, and called for 'the strongest possible sanctions against Putin's regime and its enablers'.[37])

Most Russian donors to the Tory party have a story like Chernukhin's: deep connections inside the Russian ruling elite are transmuted by money into deep connections with the British one. There are many baroque vignettes of Russians making this leap. In 2013 Putin's judo partner met the then prime minister Cameron at a fundraising event, in an encounter organised by the lobbying company founded by former Ulster Unionist MP David Burnside, which was paid by the Kremlin to promote Russia's image.[38] Putin's personal friend Gérard López, a Spanish Luxembourger, donated £400,000 to the Conservatives in 2016, in support of his friend Zac Goldsmith's run for mayor of London.[39] Lev Mikheev, a Russian-born investment banker and Tory donor, still had offices next door to the Kremlin in 2023.[40] He gave £10,000 to Rory Stewart's failed bid for Tory leader in 2019. (Stewart's campaign had capped donations at that amount, presumably to keep donors' influence under control.)[41]

One former MP, a Good Chap, told me that being in British politics this century felt like living in a John Le Carré novel. On the surface, ageing public schoolboys in suits; beneath them, the sewers. Even an alleged Russian spy was able to pay into British politics while barely causing a ripple. Dmitry Leus, born in Turkmenistan, was jailed for money laundering in Russia in 2004. He bought a home in Virginia Water in Surrey in about 2014, set up the Leus Family Foundation and began donating to the Tories. In 2021, when Dominic Raab was deputy prime minister, Leus gave £30,000 to Raab's local Conservative Association in Esher and Walton. In 2022, Labour MP Liam Byrne told the Commons that Leus had been recruited by Russia's FSB spy agency: 'There is clear knowledge of his recruitment by the FSB, who got him out of prison [in 2006]. He has a criminal record in Russia, and according to intelligence sources that I have seen, he is "absolutely dependent on the FSB".'

Leus tweeted his denial: 'I was poisoned by them [the FSB] in Lefortovo prison! They ruined my life. Strange recruitment method. Mr Byrne might want to elaborate, his intelligence sources were from within the Kremlin.'[42] Leus says his Russian conviction was later overturned; Margaret Hodge retorts that this is 'untrue'.[43]

Or take the art dealer Ehud Sheleg, who became the Tories' sole treasurer under Johnson in 2019. Two years later, reported the *New York Times*,[44] Barclays Bank alerted the National Crime Agency to suspicions around Sheleg's donation of $630,225 to the party in 2018. The source of the funds seemed to be his father-in-law Sergei Kopytov, who had been a minister in an earlier pro-Kremlin Ukrainian government of Crimea, prior to Russia's annexation of the region. The day before Sheleg made the donation, $2.5 million sent by Kopytov landed in the joint account of Sheleg and his wife.

'Kopytov can be stated with considerable certainty to have been the true source of the donation,' Barclays' alert said. A lawyer for Sheleg denied this, saying the millions that Kopytov sent him and his wife were 'entirely separate' from the gift to the Tories.[45] Barclays flagged the transaction as a potentially illegal political donation (since only British citizens are allowed to give to British parties) and also as potential money-laundering.

Money-laundering is one of the many vulnerabilities of British politics. Money-laundering checks required of banks and businesses have become stricter in recent years. A clothes boutique, say, must report any suspicious transaction of more than £10,000. But 'the regime of checks that political parties are required to undertake has stayed largely unchanged since 2001,' said the NGO Spotlight on Corruption in 2022.[46] Political parties can make voluntary reports of suspicious money flows. In practice, they don't.[47]

Anyway, it's perfectly legal for a British citizen to take money from a foreigner and use it to make a political donation. Should you receive a multi-million-pound gift from some anonymous but as yet unsanctioned offshore company, you can give it to your favourite party. The National Crime Agency and the Electoral Commission found 'no evidence' that Sheleg had committed an offence.[48] More generally, the long-term underfunding of the NCA, the Serious Fraud Office and other investigative agencies stops them taking on London's super rich and their teams of expensive lawyers.[49] Cynics might say the underfunding was deliberate.

British journalists keep digging up worrying stories about Russian money in Westminster, but it's as the Dutch-Muscovite media magnate Derk Sauer told me about Putin's Russia: 'We reveal the craziest things. And nothing happens. Deathly silence.'

The Kremlin in London

Rich Russians in London acting more or less independently were just one leg of modern Russia's influence operation. Russian diplomats (and spies masquerading as diplomats) were another. The 'diplomats' had their shortcomings: their heavy-handed aggression tended to irritate ruling-class Britons, and they lacked the access of the oligarchs. Still, some diplomats had full-time jobs seeking political influence. In 2010, for instance, Sergey Nalobin, first secretary at the Russian embassy, told Sergei Cristo, a Russian-born volunteer in Conservative campaign headquarters, that he could 'make introductions to Russian companies who would donate money to the Conservative Party'. According to Cristo, Nalobin said Putin's United Russia party wanted an official affiliation with the Tories.

Nalobin met senior Conservative politicians at exclusive fundraising events. He helped the Conservative Friends of Russia arrange its ten-day trip to Moscow and St Petersburg in 2012, funded by the Russian government. Among the delegates on that trip was Matthew Elliott, future chief executive of Vote Leave.

Years later the Foreign Office refused to renew Nalobin's visa. The *Guardian* and Russia's *The Insider* discovered that his father was a KGB general, while his brother worked for the FSB. Nalobin lived in a block of flats in Moscow so dense with spies that it was known as 'FSB House'. He eventually resurfaced in Estonia, which expelled him for espionage in 2022.[50]

A favourite venue for Russian and other foreign influence operations is the Carlton Club in St James. 'The original home of the Conservative Party before the creation of Conservative Central Office', as its website boasts, this is traditionally a sedate place populated by colonels' granddaughters, retired businessmen and Tory politicians. But in recent years their ranks have been joined by some charming foreign-accented young women, who waft about the club, establish themselves as 'normal' presences, and late in the evening can sometimes be seen gazing into a junior minister's eyes. Soon they're getting invited to Tory dinners and parties.

Sometimes the Kremlin cut out its London-based middle-women and -men, and spent its own money on influencing British politics. Day by day, much of this was done through its English-language TV channel, RT (formerly Russia Today). RT invited British politicians as paid guests to pontificate on world affairs. It made them feel important, the money was nice, and it warmed them up to Moscow.

The Kremlin also ran more ambitious influence ops. Fragments of these are documented in the 'Russia' report by parliament's non-partisan Intelligence and Security Committee. The report finally appeared in July 2020 after Johnson's government had prevented its publication before the general election of 2019. (Hillary Clinton called the delay 'inexplicable and shameful'.[51]) A former British intelligence officer told me that certain Russians in the UK may have encouraged the government's blocking.

The committee's report says, in a statement of the obvious: 'Russian influence in the UK is "the new normal", and there are a lot of Russians with very close links to Putin who are well integrated into the UK business and social scene, and accepted because of their wealth.'[52] But the report's text has so many redactions – made for security reasons – that much of it is hard to follow. For instance, the report notes 'credible open source commentary suggesting that Russia undertook influence campaigns in relation to the Scottish independence referendum in 2014 … It appears that *** what some commentators have described as potentially the first post-Soviet Russian interference in a Western democratic process.'[53]

Two years after Scotland's referendum, the Kremlin's interference in the Brexit vote may have been significant. Frankly, though, we don't know. That's partly because the British state has done its best not to know. The Intelligence and Security Committee says that when it asked MI5 for written evidence on whether Russia intervened in the Brexit referendum,

> MI5 initially provided just six lines of text. It stated that ***, before referring to academic studies.[43] This was noteworthy in terms of the way it was couched (***) and the reference to open source studies ***. The brevity was also, to us, again, indicative of the extreme caution amongst the intelligence and security Agencies at the thought that they might have any role in relation to the UK's democratic processes, and particularly one as contentious as the EU referendum.

The report continued:

> We have not been provided with any post-referendum assessment of Russian attempts at interference. This situation is in stark contrast to the US handling of allegations of Russian inter-ference in the 2016 presidential election, where an intelligence community assessment was pro-duced within two months of the vote, with an unclassified summary being made public.[54]

The former British intelligence officer told me that the main advocate inside Russia for influencing the

Brexit vote had been Igor Sergun, then chief of the military intelligence agency GRU. Millions of pounds were funnelled to pro-Leave organisations through the Isle of Man, the former officer said. But in January 2016, Sergun died suddenly (for whatever reason). That cut off the flows of Russian money.

There has still never been an official British enquiry into the Brexit referendum although there has been discussion about whether Russia had any hand in it.

If the Russians really sat out the referendum, it would have been a rare British political event that they missed. GCHQ's National Cyber Security Centre (NCSC) says Russia has targeted British MPs, including through spear phishing, since at least 2015.[55] 'The UK Government is almost certain that Russian actors sought to interfere in the 2019 general election', reported the NCSC.[56]

You might wonder: where are Britain's intelligence services in all this? Aren't they curious about foreign interests buying or subverting people in British politics? But this is where the so-called 'Wilson doctrine' comes in. Harold Wilson, as prime minister in 1966 – himself wrongly suspected by some right-wing MI5 officers of being a Soviet spy – announced that the security services wouldn't tap MPs' phones.[57] A broader convention that British spooks don't investigate British politicians holds to this day.

From the Party to parties: how the Lebedevs charmed London

Of all the Russian influencers in British politics until 2022, first prize must go to a father-and-son operation: the former KGB agent Alexander Lebedev and his son Evgeny, the newspaper proprietor. Their story exemplifies Westminster's openness to influence-buying foreigners.

Alexander Lebedev first arrived in London in 1988, as an undercover KGB man working in the Soviet embassy in Kensington Palace Gardens. Today the street is known as 'Billionaires Row', in tribute to the rich foreigners who live there, notes Paul Caruana Galizia in his revelatory podcast series on the Lebedevs for *Tortoise Media*.

Lebedev has said his only task in London was reading the newspapers for signs that capitalism was collapsing. In fact, corrects Caruana Galizia, his duties probably included monitoring British politicians.[58] At the time, Lebedev wouldn't have had much hope of influencing them.

A question plaguing the British intelligence services for decades has been: is Alexander Lebedev really a *former* KGB agent? Is there even such a thing as a former KGB agent? Putin himself has said it's impossible to leave the KGB. British officials worry much more about Alexander than Evgeny[59] – but Evgeny was the family's lead contact with its most influential friend, Boris Johnson.

Like many KGB men, Alexander Lebedev got rich from the breakup of the USSR. He founded a bank, was for a time a billionaire,[60] and moved back to London, where he made nice with the ruling elite. His main priority there was undoubtedly looking after Lebedevs. But like so many rich Russians in London, he also wanted to cover his backside in Moscow. He had fallen out with Putin before. Now he needed to manage his relationship with both the Kremlin and Westminster. And the one was a lot more demanding than the other.

Evgeny, fully bilingual, a generous host with a beautifully trimmed beard, ingratiated the Lebedevs with high-end Londoners. A guest at one of their parties, held at Princess Diana's family seat of Althorp in 2006, told Caruana Galizia: 'I walked on to the dancefloor, probably in a fairly heightened state, and I see, dancing in a circle, Orlando Bloom, Mikhail Gorbachev and Salman Rushdie. And I was like: this has got to be the most fucking surreal thing I've ever seen in my life.'[61]

In 2009, the Lebedevs bought 76 per cent of the lossmaking *Evening Standard* newspaper for £1. Alexander publicly reminisced about scouring the paper for information as a young spy.[62] According to Caruana Galizia, he had told his British business partners he would only buy the *Standard* if the Kremlin gave him permission – and he said he wanted to buy it for the benefit of Russia.[63] The Lebedevs turned the *Standard* into a freesheet, boosting circulation to 600,000.[64] A year later, they paid another £1 for the *Independent* and the *Independent on Sunday*.

The *Standard* in those days had a strong voice in London, and Evgeny Lebedev, who ran the papers, got close to the city's then mayor, Boris Johnson. 'I am proud to call him a friend,' said Johnson in 2011.[65] After one lunch, Johnson wrote to Evgeny saying he would be 'thrilled' if the *Standard* and the *Independent* covered some of his mayoral project. He said his team was 'all set to make a presentation to Geordie' [Greig, a fellow Old Etonian, then the newspapers' editorial director].[66]

In 2012, eight days before Johnson stood for re-election as mayor against Labour's Ken Livingstone, the *Standard* ran a front-page editorial headlined, 'Boris Johnson: The Right Choice for London'.[67] Two days before the vote, the *Standard* featured the following headlines:

BORIS JOHNSON: I'LL GET CAPITAL THROUGH
TOUGH TIMES WITH 200,000 JOBS

KEN LIVINGSTONE IS A 'FIGURE OF THE
PAST', SAYS CHARLES CLARKE

BUSINESS LEADERS BACK BORIS TO DRIVE RECOVERY

SLAPSTICK WILL KEEP JOHNSON SAFE FROM HUBRIS

ON BALANCE, BORIS DESERVES TO
STAY IN OFFICE – JUST[68]

Johnson won re-election with 51.5 per cent of the vote, keeping alive his national political ambitions.

Evgeny fancied himself as a journalist and essayist. This was a genuine part of his self-image, one of his former employees told me. Once, while freelancing for the BBC, Evgeny asked the Belarussian dictator Alexander Lukashenko what he thought of group sex, but he also had a serious mode, composing essays in defence of Russian foreign policy. After Putin invaded Crimea in 2014, Evgeny's piece in the *Standard* was headlined, 'To tackle Russia we have first to understand it: The West is far too ready to judge President Putin by old Cold War stereotypes.' Alexander Lebedev, writing in the *Independent*, suggested that the West should let Russia keep Crimea at least for a while.[69]

In 2015 the Russian army helped out Syria's dictator Bashar al-Assad by bombing much of his country. Evgeny's response was an article urging Britain to buddy up with Putin over Syria. In passing, he advertised his ongoing Russian power connections: 'I have no doubt, based on conversations with senior figures in Moscow, that the Kremlin wants to make an ally rather than an enemy of Britain.'[70] Johnson echoed some of Evgeny's views, blaming the EU for Russia's annexation of Crimea, and urging the UK to work with Putin.[71]

The Lebedevs' reach spread. One morning in 2017 I met an old friend for coffee at the Quaker Centre in Euston. My friend, a lovely man, is a London enabler of the foreign-born super rich. He works from a patrician address, wears fine suits, and can play up his private-school accent to impress clients. Though always law-abiding himself, he'd never be so vulgar as to ask clients if they had ever stolen, say, Russian mineral wealth.

The day we met, he was operating somewhere in the Lebedevs' orbit. Before we sat down to catch up on life, he checked his phone once more. 'They're about to appoint George Osborne as editor of the *Standard*,' he explained. Osborne, recently ejected as chancellor after Brexit, was quite a catch for rich Russians. I thought: so this is how Britain now works. In 2020, Osborne was succeeded as editor of the *Standard* by Emily Sheffield, David Cameron's sister-in-law.[72]

Meanwhile, the Lebedevs had opened a new European base at Alexander's Palazzo Terranova in Umbria, Italy. This piqued the interest of the Italian External Intelligence and Security Agency, AISE.

It reported that Alexander Lebedev had invested in property with individuals linked to the Camorra and Ndrangheta mafia clans, and that he enjoyed 'the favour and friendship of Vladimir Putin'.[73] The Italians concluded that the palazzo was being used for espionage purposes.[74]

The Lebedevs' parties at Terranova became legendary. These were intimate gatherings, with never more than about twenty guests.[75] Johnson first attended one in 2012.[76] Asked by Carole Cadwalladr what happened at the parties, Johnson's sister Rachel shrugged: 'You'll have to ask one of the men. The women are sent home at midnight.'[77]

Well, not all the women. I met a younger, beautiful, highly educated British woman who had attended at least one Terranova party. She said there were two categories of women brought in to entertain the men: posh decorative Britons like herself, there to jolly things along at table, and professional sex workers. If anyone wanted to collect *kompromat* on guests, Terranova was the perfect setting.

A spokesperson for Evgeny Lebedev has said: 'Any suggestion he was or would be party to allowing any form of espionage, whether connected to Russia or anyone else, would be false. This allegation bears the hallmarks of anti-Russian racist harassment.'[78]

The Umbrian visit that will always taint Johnson – and seems to have been a much worse security breach than the Profumo affair – happened on the last weekend of April 2018. It was a month after Russian agents had travelled to Salisbury armed with a Novichok nerve agent to try to kill Sergei Skripal, a Russian spy who had defected to Britain, and his daughter Yulia. This was merely the most shameless of Russia's murder attempts on British soil. Various other exiled Russians have died mysteriously here, such as the oligarch Boris Berezovsky, found hanging from his cashmere scarf in his ex-wife's home in Ascot, in what may have been a suicide.[79]

The Skripal attack (along with Russian cyber-attacks on the Foreign Office) expressed the Kremlin's sense of impunity in Britain. But this attack was outrageous enough to damage relations with the West. NATO countries reacted by expelling hundreds of Russian diplomats.

Alexander Lebedev reportedly offered to repair the damage by acting as a back-channel between Johnson, then Britain's foreign secretary, and Putin. It would have been a way for the KGB Old Boy to make himself useful to Moscow. Foreign Office officials rejected the idea.[80] But Johnson didn't.

On 27 April 2018 he attended a NATO summit in Brussels where he urged fellow foreign ministers to do more to counter Russia. From Brussels, he flew straight to the Palazzo Terranova, unaccompanied by either civil servants or his security detail.

It was rumoured for years that Johnson met Alexander Lebedev at the palazzo that weekend. Only in 2022 did he finally confirm this. Facing the Liaison Select Committee of MPs the day before he announced his resignation as prime minister, he blustered at first. Finally, questioned by the Labour MP Meg Hillier, he admitted to an undocumented meeting with the longtime KGB agent at the man's family property without British officials present. Johnson said,

> 'On the occasion you're mentioning, if that was when I was foreign secretary, then yes.'
> 'Without officials?', Hillier asked.
> 'Yes. That, that makes sense, yes.'
> 'Did you report to your officials that you had met him?'
> 'Ahhh – I think I did mention it, yes.'
> Later he added: 'I met him, in Italy, as it happens.'

Johnson said (offering a peculiar caveat) that 'as far as I am aware, no Government business was discussed'. It had just been 'a private, social occasion'.[81] He never logged the encounter in the Foreign Office's registry of ministerial meetings.[82]

During that same Umbrian visit, one source told Caruana Galizia, Alexander Lebedev tried to set up a direct unmonitored call between Johnson and Russia's foreign minister Sergei Lavrov to discuss the Skripal affair. Three people 'connected to the Foreign Office' supported the source's allegation, reports Caruana Galizia.

It would normally be unthinkable for a British foreign secretary to have a sensitive discussion with a minister of a hostile power alone and unprepared, without officials. Yet Johnson seems to have agreed to it, perhaps feeling that with the Lebedevs, he was among friends. In the event, says Caruana Galizia, the conversation with Lavrov didn't happen because Johnson overslept – or possibly pretended to oversleep, belatedly realising the risks to himself of taking the call. When the story broke near the end of his premiership, Downing Street didn't deny it.

Johnson left Evgeny's palazzo on Sunday 29 April 2018. He was photographed by tourists at Perugia airport, alone, looking hungover, almost as if he had slept in his suit. His only luggage appeared to be a thick book on war strategy. In his register of hospitality, he declared he had made the visit with 'a spouse, family member or friend', reportedly a woman – but who was that person, and why didn't they fly back with him?[83]

Eighteen months later, Alexander Lebedev told the *Spectator* magazine that western media coverage of Russia was 'pure darkness. It's just not fair. It wasn't the Russian people who poisoned Skripal. It was just a few guys.'[84]

None of this dented Johnson's relationship with the Lebedevs. Very soon after becoming prime minister, he nominated Evgeny for a peerage. The *Standard*, newspaper of a generally Labour-supporting city, still had Johnson's back. The night after he won the 2019 general election (and hugged Ben Elliot), he attended Alexander's sixtieth birthday party, which featured caviar and a Corbyn impersonator.[85] British Russianists were watching the Lebedev–Johnson relationship, one of them told me, with 'our hair on fire'.

In March 2020, when Johnson belatedly realised that Covid-19 had struck, his first thoughts seem to have been for Evgeny. On 18 March, the day Johnson announced that all schools were closing, he had a twenty-five-minute phone call with Evgeny and a three-minute conversation with his health secretary Matt Hancock, reported Josiah Mortimer in *Byline Times*.[86]

The day after, Johnson and Evgeny met for forty-one minutes. Johnson's message to Britons to work from home 'if you can' had plunged the perennially hard-up *Standard* into crisis. Without commuters, its circulation would collapse. Then the ads that accounted for more than 90 per cent of the freesheet's revenues would melt away.[87]

The time had come for Johnson to return the

favour for the Lebedevs' long-term support. The government had allocated an advertising budget for messaging about Covid-19, which, writes Mortimer 'funnelled hundreds of millions of subsidies in the form of Government advertising into a select group of newspapers'. Evgeny wanted a slice of it. Johnson agreed to help him out.[88] Soon afterwards, the government also scrapped the usual 20 per cent VAT charge on digital news sites.[89]

Johnson's then chief adviser Dominic Cummings tweeted two years later: 'The newspapers negotiated direct bungs to themselves with him [Johnson], no officials on calls, then he told officials to send the £ – dressed up as "covid relief" etc'.[90] Cummings told the Covid-19 inquiry: 'There were specific concerns and also suspicions of possible corruption in terms of his relationship with [the *Standard*'s editor] Osborne, and funnelling money to the *Evening Standard*.'[91]

The *Standard* was suitably grateful. On 28 April 2020 Hancock Whatsapped Osborne, his former colleague: 'I need to call in a favour tomorrow.' He wanted a helpful front-page story on Covid testing. Osborne agreed.[92]

All the while, Johnson was pushing forward the application for Evgeny's peerage. The House of Lords Appointment Committee (HOLAC) opposed it, warning in a letter that Evgeny's 'familial links' created risks to national security. The Channel 4 programme *Dispatches* said intelligence officials briefed Johnson in Downing Street, trying to change his mind over the peerage. Then – in a probably unprecedented move – the officials contacted Buckingham Palace, hoping to persuade the Queen to block it. She declined.[93] The government refused to publish the intelligence services' advice.[94] The spooks seem finally to have given up the struggle.

Evgeny and Johnson rolled out their habitual defence whenever the Lebedevs came under scrutiny: it was just racism. Johnson told officials in the Cabinet Office that the security advice was 'anti-Russianism'.[95] When *Private Eye* magazine noted that Evgeny's grandfather had served in Stalin's cabinet, Evgeny sent a 5 a.m. email to the editor that began, 'Dear Racist Cunt'.[96] He wrote an article complaining about

> the snobbery and casual racism which is still widespread throughout British society – even in surprising places. This is a racism that considers the House of Lords to be no place for someone such as me.
>
> Take, for example, the extensive coverage of me in the *Guardian*, that beacon of tolerance, over the past 12 months, where stories invariably describe me as 'Russian' or 'Russian-born' in their first sentences.[97]

He must have understood that the critics weren't anti-Russian. They were anti-KGB. Evgeny's birthplace was irrelevant. What mattered was that his money and his newspapers came from his father, a KGB Old Boy who still seemed connected to Putin's regime.

Evgeny got his peerage. Late in 2020, he became Baron Lebedev of Hampton in the London Borough of Richmond upon Thames and of Siberia in the Russian Federation.

On 17 February 2022, while Russian troops were massing on Ukraine's borders, the Conservative government finally scrapped its 'golden visa' scheme. It admitted later that ten recipients of golden visas were subsequently sanctioned Russian oligarchs.[98]

A week later, Putin's army poured into Ukraine. The war cast fresh light on an almost unnoticed episode of eleven months earlier: a Russian-owned firm, Megahertz, had installed a new press briefing room at 9 Downing Street. Megahertz's parent company was OKNO-TV, which had also performed technical work for Russia's state-run broadcaster RT. Megahertz's activity in Downing Street 'included installing computers, cameras, microphones and a control desk,' reported *The Times*. Allegra Stratton, Johnson's short-lived press secretary, had said there were 'absolutely not' any security concerns.[99]

Evgeny understood at once that Russia's invasion

would end his family's ability to straddle London and Moscow. He appealed to Putin 'to stop Russians killing their Ukrainian brothers and sisters.'[100] Putin didn't listen.

The Lebedevs' good times in London were over. Alexander cut his ties with the *Independent*.[101] Johnson's government didn't sanction him, perhaps worried about what he might reveal, but Canada did, listing him among fourteen people who 'directly enabled Vladimir Putin's senseless war in Ukraine'.

Britain's institutions jettisoned Evgeny. He lamented in a self-pitying screed, written while Russian soldiers were massacring Ukrainians:

> Most ludicrous of all is the Royal Horticultural Society, which had previously bent over backwards for me to attend events and enjoyed the support of the *Evening Standard*. This year, it refused to give me passes to the press launch of the Hampton Court Flower Show.[102]

He had discovered that all those years, he had never really been 'one of us'. The ruling caste had been sniggering behind his back. I am told he feels betrayed by the Tories. Years pass without his setting foot in the House of Lords.[103]

Even after Russia's full invasion, the Conservatives continued to accept money from donors with direct or indirect links to the Russian economy, notably from Chernukhin.[104] But here's the great paradox: the party that had taken so much money from Russians stood unambiguously against Putin's Russia. The British government's response to Russia's invasion of 2022 was firm. More than France and Germany, Britain had also supported Ukraine after Putin's first invasion in 2014, even if it did little to help. This illustrates the complicated dance the Tories conducted for a decade with Kremlin-connected London Russians. The party was nice to rich London Russians, yet tough on Russia. I asked Rodric Braithwaite, former British ambassador to Moscow, a nearly lifelong student of Russia, now in his nineties, to explain the paradox. He replied that Britain in general, and the Conservative Party in particular, had been hostile to an authoritarian Russia for centuries. He added: 'We were allied with the Russians in several wars, especially against Napoleon and Hitler, but the alliances were always pretty tetchy.'

The Tories never went in for the Putinphilia displayed by politicians like Donald Trump, Nigel Farage, Marine Le Pen, Viktor Orbán, Gerhard Schröder and Matteo Salvini. British public opinion probably wouldn't have accepted it anyway.

In short, the Kremlin's attempts to buy influence in London may not have succeeded – except, possibly, in the unexamined case of Brexit. The joke among some Tory MPs in 2022 was, 'The Conservative Party is very ungrateful.'

However, the party was grateful to individual rich Russians. These people, not Putin, were the chief beneficiaries of the long Russian influence operation in the UK. Until Putin finally went too far in 2022, no matter how many countries Russia attacked, no matter how many times it attacked people in Britain itself, the Conservative government barely ever sanctioned or barred or even investigated the wealth of[105] the small group of Russians who did so much to fund the party.

5

LONDON AFTER RUSSIA

I consider London to be the capital of the world.

Sir Mohamed Mansour, former Egyptian
government minister under the autocrat
Hosni Mubarak, and senior treasurer
of the Tory party since 2022.[1]

Britain's game-plan after February 2022 was to make
a grand gesture by kicking some rich Russians out
of London, while continuing to serve the wealthy
of almost every other country. In fact, booting out
Russians simply created a need for rich foreigners to
replace them. The American Todd Boehly bought
Roman Abramovich's football club, Chelsea.

Many rich London Russians relocated to Istanbul
and especially Dubai. After 2022, Russia became yes-
terday's problem in British political corruption. The
Russians had been the pioneers. They demonstrated
proof of concept: foreign money could buy an entrée
into British power. Now rich people tied to other
autocratic regimes – along with one or two regimes

themselves, operating without middle-men – have adopted the Russian strategy.

The most direct, like-for-like replacements of rich Russians are rich 'Gulfies' – from Qatar, the United Arab Emirates and especially Saudi Arabia. The Gulfies tend to be less interested than the Russians in acquiring a place in London society. They're after a quieter kind of influence. In 2017 and 2018, the Saudi investor Sultan Mohamed Abuljadayel bought about 30 per cent of the *Standard* and *Independent* newspapers from the Lebedevs. The buyer initially shielded his identity in the modern London way, behind a Cayman Islands company. The *FT* reported that Abuljadayel was 'associated' with the investment banking arm of Saudi Arabia's National Commercial Bank, which is majority owned by the Saudi state's Public Investment Fund (PIF).[2]

The British government launched an investigation into the sale of the newspapers in 2019, enquiring whether their editorial independence would be compromised. Lebedev's lawyers tried to stop the investigation, arguing that the government had missed the deadline to intervene. The government replied that it was acting late in part because both Lebedev and the Saudi investors had refused to provide important information. A court hearing was told that Abuljadayel had fronted a series of 'unconventional, complex, and clandestine' deals for the newspapers, and that the *Standard* and *Independent* didn't know who ultimately employed him.[3] The sale went ahead regardless, though culture secretary Nicky Morgan expressed concern that the *Independent*'s publishers and Lebedev Holdings Ltd had not fully clarified the ultimate beneficial owner of the shares.[4]

The purchase of the newspapers was just one example of Gulf state-linked entities buying British mindshare. Saudis also spend generously with London public relations firms. And the Saudi government throws consulting gigs to British ex-politicians, such as former chancellor Philip Hammond, former minister Francis Maude and of course Tony Blair.[5] The financial intertwining of Gulf and British elites that began with Al Yamamah forty years ago is hitting new heights of sophistication. Gulf money now pervades elite London, but often so unobtrusively as to go unnoticed. One example: the excellent academic discussion titled 'Money and Politics: analysing donations to UK political parties, 2000–2021', an important source for this book, took place in the London School of Economics Sheikh Zayed Theatre, a room named after the first president of the United Arab Emirates.[6]

Looking ahead, you might reasonably forecast that the rising state in the league table of London political influence will be China. Certainly, there have already been minor flurries over Chinese interference. Li Xuelin, a senior member of the Chinese Communist Party, who became Lady Bates through marrying a former Tory minister, gave the Conservatives almost £200,000.[7]

In January 2022, MI5 warned that an agent for China's Communist Party, named as the London-based solicitor Christine Ching Kui Lee, was accused of 'facilitating financial donations to serving and aspiring politicians' on behalf of foreign nationals based in Hong Kong and China. The agency said Lee had donated more than £420,000 to the Labour MP Barry Gardiner, former shadow secretary for international trade. MI5 urged anyone whom Lee contacted to be 'mindful of her affiliation with the Chinese state and [her] remit to advance the CCP's agenda in UK politics'. Lee and China's foreign ministry both denied the allegations. Gardiner, who had employed Lee's son, said he had been 'liaising with our security services for a number of years about her'.

Then, in 2023, the Metropolitan Police arrested Chris Cash, a 28-year-old British parliamentary researcher suspected of spying for China. Cash had worked for the China Research Group of MPs, and subsequently for Alicia Kearns, chair of the Commons foreign affairs committee.[8] He and another man were charged with espionage offences in April 2024.[9]

Chinese intelligence services 'target the UK and its interests prolifically and aggressively,' warned parliament's Intelligence and Security Committee in 2023.[10] The Chinese Communist Party posed 'the most game-changing strategic challenge to the UK', said Ken McCallum, director general of MI5.[11] China certainly has far more resources than Russia to run British influence ops. It could easily, for instance, groom a couple of dozen young wannabe MPs, help them get selected as parliamentary candidates for Labour and the Tories, and then assist their rise up the party ladders, perhaps all the way to Downing Street. China also has the advantage of not alienating Britons quite as blatantly as Putin does. Whereas Russia tries to blow up western systems, China prefers just orienting them to its interests.

Yet there's reason to doubt that China will become the new Russia of British politics. One Sinologist warned me not to overestimate Chinese savvy. After all, he asked, what had been the point in cultivating a 'clapped-out opposition MP' like Gardiner? The expert said China often misidentified the weak spots of western political systems – though it had done better in Australia and Canada than in the UK. Russia was more sure-footed in London, partly because rich Russians living there could explain the place to the Kremlin. There were fewer rich Chinese interpreters of Britain.

Lastly, London looms less large on China's map of the world than it did on Russia's map. The UK just doesn't matter much to Beijing. Britain won't be a major factor in any struggle over Taiwan or economic measures against China. Victor Gao, a spokesman for the Chinese Communist Party, put this succinctly in an interview with LBC radio in 2023, when he dismissed the notion that the UK should regard China as an enemy or competitor:

> What do China and Britain compete with? China is the largest manufacturer of automobiles. Competing with Britain? No ... China will be the most important producer and R&D in terms of semiconductors in no time. Does that mean China competes with Britain? No. China will be the leading nation in AI revolution. Is Britain a competitor? No. So I think British government should not overestimate its impact on the global scene, and view Britain as a rival of China ... China is a fact, China is a megatrend for Britain to live with and get along with.[12]

It seems, then, that the Russian-led phalanx that infiltrated the British elite between about 2008 and 2022 will be replaced by a more diverse array of foreign actors. The Gulf states may take the lead, but there will also be a random assortment of rich individuals

from everywhere. Think of the Kenyan-born international telecoms dealmaker Mohamed Amersi, who
we encountered in Chapter Three: the Tory donor
and client of Ben Elliot's Quintessentially who scored
a dinner with the then Prince Charles.

Amersi tried to create a group to oversee the Tory
party's Middle East relations, to be called Conservative Friends of the Middle East and North Africa.
It was to displace the party's four-decade-old Middle
East liaison group, the Conservative Middle East
Council. Ben Elliot, as Tory party co-chair, talked to
the Saudi and Bahraini ambassadors about Amersi's
plans. He didn't disclose that Amersi was his paying
client at Quintessentially.[13] An email sent to the Tories'
head of fundraising, Mike Chattey, and three other
party officials on 25 February 2020 noted that Amersi's Friends group, 'to be fair, would have some of the
best group fund raising potential if done right'.[14]

That was undoubtedly true. What's also true,
says a former intelligence officer, is that a Conservative international liaison group like this is 'a national
security asset'. It sits in the soft underbelly of British
democracy. You have to be careful who runs it.

So is Amersi just a public-spirited believer in
Brexit? Well, as he himself said in a talk in Oxford:
'Political donors are not philanthropists. They expect
something in return.'[15]

Amersi is a tricky person to write about, because

he has a habit of suing anyone who does.[16] Happily, when he tried that on Labour's Margaret Hodge, the Conservative MP David Davis came to her aid. On 29 June 2023, Davis used parliamentary privilege to tell the Commons about Amersi's 'long history of involvement in corruption, in bribery and in buying access to politicians.' Amersi, said Davis,

> ... is a wealthy businessman who made large sums of money in Russia, Uzbekistan, Kazakhstan and Nepal ... In 2005, Amersi made $4 million arranging the acquisition of a Russian telecoms company on behalf of a company he knew was secretly owned by a powerful Putin ally, the then Russian telecoms minister, Leonid Reiman ...
>
> In the UK, Amersi used his fortune to gain access to powerful people. He coined the term 'access capitalism', describing his own attempts to gain access to the royal household and Ministers, with payments to Prince Charles's charities and the Conservative Party. He and his partner gave £750,000 to the Conservative Party, and he makes no bones about what he thought he was buying.
>
> ... a joint investigation by the BBC and the *Guardian* revealed that he profited from a corrupt deal involving the Swedish energy company Telia, and a high-profile kleptocrat in Uzbekistan ...
>
> Amersi helped to facilitate a $220 million

purchase of shares from a shell company owned
by the daughter of the Uzbek President at the
time. That share purchase was in fact a concealed
bribe – that was the clear view of the US Department of Justice ...[17]

Not three weeks after Davis's speech, Amersi
co-hosted the annual diplomatic party of the Conservative Foreign and Commonwealth Council at the
House of Lords.[18] He has said that 'not a penny' of the
money he made in Russia funded his British political
donations.[19] His lawyers denied that he 'knowingly'
facilitated corrupt payments.[20]

Soon after Davis's speech, Amersi seems to have
gone off the Tories. He commented on an article
about their top ten donors (which didn't include
him): 'If this is true we do not have a government
of the people, by the people and for the people but
instead of the rich, by the rich and for the rich!'[21] He
also fell out with Ben Elliot.[22]

Like Evgeny Lebedev before him, Amersi had
discovered that he wasn't one of us. The Tories had
just pretended to like him. He really ought to have
worked this out earlier. If you have to give people
money in order to meet them, it's a clue that they
didn't want to meet you.

As I write, the figure with foreign autocratic connections who is closest to the heart of Toryism is

probably Sir Mohamed Mansour (knighted by Sunak in 2024). Anyone from any other national political tradition would find it remarkable that the Conservative Party's senior treasurer is a former Egyptian transport minister under dictator Hosni Mubarak. 'I did not believe that Mubarak was a bad man,' Mansour says of the corrupt autocratic torturer.[23]

Mansour is the billionaire head of the Mansour Group conglomerate, which was founded by his father. In 2009 Mansour left Egypt for Britain, where he became a citizen. Like Amersi,[24] he lives in a townhouse in Mayfair; Mansour's is worth about £28 million. He began donating to the Tories in 2016 through his company Unatrac. He was represented by the communications firm Hawthorn Advisors, co-founded by Ben Elliot.

In 2022 Mansour became the Conservative Party's senior treasurer – effectively, its lead fundraiser. Around the same time, he reached a multimillion-pound settlement with HMRC over previously unpaid corporation tax.

In 2023 it emerged that Unatrac was still supplying Russia's oil and gas industry despite the sanctions imposed after the invasion of Ukraine. Unatrac said its operations in Russia were then suspended.[25] Soon afterwards, the future Lord Mansour (Tory treasurers become peers the way tadpoles become frogs) gave the Conservatives £5 million.

Imagine, again, the peer-group effect on politicians of hanging out with people like this. Senior Tories start to absorb the billionaire's view of the world. No wonder Sunak flies around Britain by helicopter or private jet: the plutocrats he consorts with, including his own in-laws, don't use trains either. One of his roundtrips to Wales by private jet was paid for by 'a minor Tory donor called Akhil Tripathi, co-founder of a heavily lossmaking start-up that hopes to sell an anti-snoring device to the NHS,' wrote the *FT*. In April 2024 the High Court froze £14 million of the Indian-born Tripathi's assets, including his townhouse in Belgravia, over fraud allegations involving his start-up.[26]

But Sunak can afford to fund rides out of his own pocket.[27] Many people can in the circles he frequented before politics. Likewise, his peer group would have understood his wife's long-time non-domiciled status, and the couple's trusts registered in Caribbean tax havens even while he was chancellor overseeing British taxes, and his own possession of an American green card until 2021, which required him privately to declare himself a permanent resident of the US.[28] After all, billionaires tend to have international lives, and to opt out of national tax systems.

In Sunak's world, foreign investment is almost always a good thing. And the Tory party had become reliant on it. It wasn't about to limit foreign-linked political donations. In 2023, several peers who were alumni of the security services, including MI5's former director general Jonathan Evans, backed an amendment to the National Security Bill that would have forced parties to verify the true source of political donations. This would have at least shrunk one of the many loopholes that let foreign money into the system. The government whipped its MPs into voting down the amendment.[29] Today, if you're a British cat charity and you receive a suspect donation, you have to ascertain its origins. If you're a political party, not so much.

The 2024 general election will see the tide of murky foreign money reach record heights. That's partly because the government has extended the lifelong right to vote to 3.4 million Britons living abroad – including me. I'm personally pleased. I've re-registered as a voter with the local council where I lived until 2002.

But the extension creates risks, too: here is an opportunity for people living abroad who aren't British to try to sign up for the electoral register, and then make donations. They won't need to show photo ID. They'll just need to ask an existing British voter to vouch for their identity. If the donor is subsequently exposed as non-British, well, their money will already have done its job, and nobody is ever likely to punish them. Susan Hawley, of the Spotlight on Corruption charity said the government was 'leaving the integrity of our next general election at serious risk.'[30] You'd almost think the government didn't mind.

6

LABOUR: A REQUIEM FOR THE UNION BARON

Same old story – Labour in
hock to union paymasters
Daily Express headline, 21 September 2020[1]

Gary Lubner, the businessman who is giving Labour about £5 million ahead of the general election, is sitting in his beautiful airy office in the West End. It's a minute's walk from the offices of Quintessentially, Ben Elliot's luxury international concierge firm that partially morphed into the Conservative Party's fundraising operation. This is the London that the cheery, pixie-like Lubner inhabits: just two miles from Westminster but in a different money zone. He was still out when I arrived, so staff members brought me to the basement café, where a sort of inhouse barista served me the perfect espresso. One of Lubner's advisers sat with me until the secretary summoned us.

Lubner grew up Jewish in South Africa. His

grandfather founded a glass company, but Lubner was also raised on the story of his grandmother, who as a child had seen her parents shot in front of her in a Lithuanian pogrom. She'd been lucky to be able to make a new life in South Africa. Lubner grew up caring about refugees and migrants.

He himself migrated to the UK around 1990, keeping his South African accent. In Britain he eventually funded about a hundred migrant charities and NGOs. If his grandparents had come here now, he told me, they would be 'in some detention centre, waiting to be sent to Rwanda.' After he'd spent about four weeks studying British migrant issues, he realised: 'The only way we can make the difference is by changing the government.' He began donating to Keir Starmer's Labour.

Lubner had the means. He had grown what was originally the family company, Belron, into a multinational behemoth, which owns the car-glass-repair brand Autoglass. 'It was just an ordinary fucking windscreen company and it became a remarkable story,' he told me. He stepped down as chief executive in 2023, with Belron worth (he told me) £21 billion.

He said he took 'very little credit' for the company's success. Still, he benefited from what he called 'highly leveraged incentive schemes'. [2] He realised he would soon have 'obscene amounts of money.' He said, 'I felt very uncomfortable with it. I knew I would never give my kids that amount of wealth, mainly because they didn't want it.' Sure, he'd worked hard, but so had nurses and teachers.[3] He felt better after deciding to give away '80, 90 per cent-plus of my wealth'. The money he was donating to Labour was 'a fraction of my giving'. He donates much more in South Africa.

He had hoped to give to Labour anonymously. 'Donor', he pointed out, had become a 'loaded term' in British politics after all the scandals. Then he learned that legally he had to donate under his own name. 'By the way,' he added, 'I agree with that. I knew when I was going to be donating that I would get all this shit coming my way, but I've come to terms with it. In a perfect world I don't think there should be any bloody donations to political parties. In some countries the state does that.'

He visited Labour's senior people, and couldn't believe how little staff support they had – nothing like the 35,000 employees he had at Belron. ('The idea that you can run everything yourself as the CEO is complete bullshit.') When he visited shadow chancellor Rachel Reeves, he discovered that she shared her small office with her chief of staff. Halfway through the meeting, Reeves apologised, went online, and began trying to buy a train ticket to Leeds. Lubner was astounded: senior people in business didn't book their own travel. He asked her what she would need to spend her time thinking great thoughts about the economy instead. He ended up paying for aides for her and other Labour frontbenchers including David Lammy (who as shadow foreign secretary had to cover the entire world part-time, when not voting or tending to his constituency). The party was pathetically grateful for Lubner's money. One senior Labour figure told him, 'I want to give you a hug!'

Labour, cash-starved since the end of New Labour, is rediscovering the phenomenon of big donors. Lubner said: 'I know all of the major Labour donors. There are not a lot of us. There should be fewer of us.' These people are virtually unknown to the public, yet they are key players in the making of the probable next government. To understand Starmer's Labour Party, you have to know who funds it.

*

The eternal cliché about Labour is that it's 'in hock to the union barons'. Indeed, until Blair became leader, Labour always got more money from trade unions than from private donors. Unions remained the party's main contributors even through much of the New Labour era.[4] The party's eleven affiliated unions pay Labour 'affiliation fees'[5] (today, typically £3 per union member) plus optional extra donations.

Corbyn as leader was particularly dependent on union money. That's largely because his far-left economic policies and the party's eruptions of anti-semitism frightened off Labour's few remaining donors.[6] In 2016 the *Mail on Sunday* gleefully ran an article headlined, '"Why I despise Jeremy Corbyn and his Nazi stormtroopers", by Jewish Labour donor Michael Foster'.[7] Lubner's youngest son was a Labour student activist, and when they'd go to party meetings together during the Corbyn era, Lubner saw him get 'abused, pilloried, attacked'. Lubner told my *FT* colleague George Parker: 'I was horrified by what was going on.'[8]

The emblematic Labour donor to check out during Corbynism was David Sainsbury. The quiet, unassuming supermarket heir is somewhat ironi-cally referred to as 'Big Dave'. He joined Labour in the 1960s, inherited a large shareholding aged just twenty-six, and over the nearly six decades since has become the first Briton to donate £1 billion to charity.[9]

Sainsbury split from Labour when it turned left in the early 1980s, jumping with other defectors to the new Social Democratic Party. He returned to Labour under Blair, who put him in the Lords and made him science minister. In 2006, Sainsbury apologised after 'unintentionally' failing to tell his top civil servant that he had lent Labour £2 million.[10] Otherwise, though, he was an unobtrusive figure. Those around him knew him as a 'benign billionaire', with his non-partisan passion for better financial management systems in government.

When Labour moved leftwards again from 2010, Sainsbury didn't make a noisy fuss. He just repeated his desertion of the 1980s and stopped his donations. Instead, using four different aliases, he gave a total of £8 million to different entities in the Remain campaign before the Brexit referendum.[11]

The quiet headquarters for anti-Corbynites within Corbyn's Labour Party was the deliberately obscure group Labour Together. For years it didn't even have a website or a Twitter account. Its offices in Vauxhall had a pirate flag on the wall, signifying its dissident status within Corbyn's party.[12] Most of my information about the group comes from reports in the *Financial Times* and *Sunday Times*, produced by the human machines that are Jim Pickard and Gabriel Pogrund and their respective colleagues Lucy Fisher, Anna Gross and Harry Yorke.[13]

Labour Together's long-term aim was to dislodge Corbyn and drag Labour back to the centre-left. In 2017, Morgan McSweeney, who had been raised in a small town in Ireland and was inspired to join Labour by the Good Friday Agreement, became the group's first full-time director. He began raising money, from two anti-Corbyn donors in particular.

One was Martin Taylor, who on paper had the identikit profile of a Tory donor: he was a Mayfair-based hedge-fund manager whose main fund, Nevsky Capital, which had been launched in the Cayman Islands, invested in big Russian companies including Gazprom and Lukoil.[14] After Taylor's belated unmasking as a major Labour donor – it took a while to identify him, because his name was so common – he explained himself in an article in Lebedev's *Independent*:

> I am a born and bred Londoner, who also happens to be a Hedge Fund manager. And I am proud to support the Labour Party. This may seem a bit odd to many people. It is commonly believed that everyone in the financial sector supports the Conservative Party, in a quest to pay ever lower levels of tax.

Taylor added that his father had been a Labour councillor and his mother the headteacher of a comprehensive school.[15] He had recently retired, aged forty-six (before un-retiring later). He first donated to Labour Together a month after Corbyn became party leader. Taylor's donations to the group soon totalled in six figures.[16]

Labour Together's second big funder was Trevor Chinn, a Jewish community leader who had inherited his father's garages and bought the Royal Automobile Club. Other rich Labour backers, such as Lord Myners and Lord Hollick, also gave to Labour Together. McSweeney initially reported their contributions to the Electoral Commission in the usual way.[17]

These men, like Lubner, inhabited the same plutocratic London as the Tory donors but they had different motivations. They weren't buccaneers who had become political donors hoping to slash taxes and regulations. If that's what they had wanted, they would have given to the Tories. Nor were they tied to foreign autocracies.

However, Labour's donors weren't far-left Corbynites either. That's why they gave to Labour Together, rather than to the main party. These people were somewhere on the broad centre-left. Just as Tory donors try to push the Conservative Party to the free-market right in their battle against rival forces within Toryism, Labour donors try to push their own party towards the centre.

The donations to Labour Together kept coming. Yet in December 2017, write Pogrund and Yorke, McSweeney, who acted as company secretary, stopped reporting them. That was despite the Electoral Commission emailing him on 6 December to tell him that Labour Together, as a members' association, was obliged to declare donations.

Why didn't he? The *Telegraph* reports that Labour

Together wanted to shield Chinn from the 'growing' anti-semitism inside Corbyn's Labour.[18] It was also a time when Corbyn, basking in an unexpectedly strong performance at the general election of May 2017, appeared untouchable. Nobody inside Labour wanted to be seen to challenge him. Over a two-year period, McSweeney registered just one gift (of £12,500 from Chinn), failing to report donations worth £730,000. This omission was a clear breach of the law.[19]

Ahead of the 2019 election Sainsbury gave £8 million to the Liberal Democrats. At the time, this was the largest donation in British political history.[20] The Lib Dems would end up with eleven seats – evidence that donations by themselves don't win elections. The shadow chancellor, John McDonnell, urged Labour to expel Sainsbury.[21]

Corbyn fought that election almost entirely funded by trade unions, which gave Labour more than £5 million. The Unite union, in particular, had a lot of say in picking a far-left slate of candidates for marginal seats.[22] Labour received just £360,000 from individuals and companies combined. Johnson's Tories raised £19.4 million for the election from donors[23] – more than fifty times as much as Labour. The Conservatives also retained a significant donation advantage from previous years.

Corbyn stepped down after leading Labour to

its smallest haul of seats since 1935.[24] Starmer began running for leader with McSweeney as his campaign manager, even though Labour Together at this point was still maintaining the pretence that it wasn't supporting any candidate. Starmer, who had become an MP only in 2015, was an uncharismatic newbie with barely any base within the party. He needed Labour Together more than it needed him.

He refused to disclose all his donors during the leadership campaign. Desperate to win over Labour members, he ran to the left, and ended up pledging to nationalise rail, mail, energy and water. Many members would have been appalled to know about the capitalists funding him. Taylor, Chinn, Hollick and Myners gave £205,000 between them, or 30 per cent of Starmer's cash donations. Starmer easily outraised the rival candidates. Quite legally, he reported the vast majority of his donations only after his victory in April 2020. He ditched most of the promised nationalisations later.[25]

As soon as Starmer became leader, McSweeney moved from Labour Together to become his new chief of staff. It was McSweeney who would select the next Labour generation of MPs, vetting most of the new candidates for parliament in the coming general election. Labour Together came out as fairly leftist on economics, and more conservative on social values.[26] It morphed into Starmer's 'policy shop': an adjunct to the leader's office, producing ideas for government. If Labour is elected, several of the group's original figures, such as Reeves, Wes Streeting and Lisa Nandy, will form the core of Starmer's cabinet.[27]

Hannah O'Rourke succeeded McSweeney as Labour Together's administrator, and discovered his years-long failure to declare donations. She belatedly registered them. The group's apology blamed 'human error and administrative oversight', but without, note Pogrund and Yorke, even mentioning that the erring human appeared to be the man now installed at the new leader's side, McSweeney.

The Electoral Commission found that Labour Together had committed over twenty separate breaches of the law involving about £700,000 in donations.[28] In the tradition of feeble British regulators of campaign finance, the Commission imposed a fine of £14,250 – equivalent to about 2 per cent of the undeclared donations. The website Business Insider seems to have been the only publication that even reported the punishment at the time.[29] McSweeney sailed on untouched.

*

Starmer as leader set about dragging Labour back to the centre. There was an obvious vacancy there. The post-Brexit Tories had done what they could to alienate business. That gave Labour a chance to replace them in the affections of corporate Britain. Starmer also understood that he would have a much easier time rebuilding the party machine and running election campaigns with policies that donors liked. He began courting London's money. At first, he and Reeves visited businesspeople in their offices. After a while, wrote my *FT* colleagues Parker and Pickard, the businesspeople began coming to them.[30]

The Tories had nearly doubled spending limits for the general election to £35 million per party on the assumption that it would help them most. That initially seemed a no-brainer. Labour was still so cash-strapped in 2021 that it accepted applications for voluntary redundancy from a reported eighty-one staff members.[31] But the new increased spending limits spurred on Labour's fundraising. As time went on, the party's financial model started to resemble that of the Tories. Labour may well succeed in raising the maximum £35 million for the 2024 election.

Lubner would have liked his donations to be spent on 'long-term thinking' about how to remake the country. He wanted to pay to train Labour's front bench in emotional intelligence and leadership skills: 'I come in thinking, "Well brilliant, I'm sure this is all in place in politics! Well, guess what?"'

But he had discovered one thing about politics: 'It's really short-term. They have to respond to this morning's headlines.' He accepted that long-term planning was pointless if you didn't win power, so most of his money was being spent on the election. Among other things, he was supporting the campaigns of over one hundred constituency candidates, at between £5,000 and £25,000 a pop.

Another of Labour's new donors was Dale Vince. A one-time New Age traveller, Vince had been living in an old army truck when he started out as a green entrepreneur. He once told the *FT*: 'Business is a sad waste of life, on the whole, and the free market's an oxymoron.' By 2024, his green-electricity company Ecotricity had made him about £100 million.

Vince was expected to give Labour £5 million ahead of the general election, ranking him up there with Lubner and Sainsbury – though his ability to come through with the cash depended on his estranged wife Kate. Her solicitor talked during the couple's divorce proceedings about trying to stop Vince donating 'what we don't want him to donate'.[32] Vince told the *FT* that he believed Labour would 'wean us off fossil fuels.' He grew so attached to the party that he even stopped marching with Just Stop Oil after the Tories began raising his connection with the radical group to embarrass Labour.[33]

Union money had been relegated to the second tier in Starmer's Labour. A traditional Tory caricature during the rail strikes of January 2023 showed him in the pocket of Mick Lynch, head of the National Union of Rail, Maritime and Transport Workers (RMT).[34] But the cliché was out of date. The RMT was no longer even affiliated with Labour. True, the union donated about £320,000 between 2010 and 2022[35] – but that was about an eighth of what Lubov Chernukhin by herself gave the Tories in the same period. In total in 2022, Labour had reported only £5.34 million in union affiliations, compared with £10.5 million in donations.[36] If Starmer was in anyone's pocket now, it was attached to a tailored silk shirt.

Labour's donations really took off in 2023, as the election loomed into view. David Sainsbury's daughter Fran Perrin, who had once been an adviser in Blair's Downing Street, became the party's biggest female donor ever, giving £1 million.[37] In the second quarter of the year, Labour's haul of over £10.4 million (a new party record) included £3 million from Sainsbury and £2.2 million from Lubner. For comparison, the general workers' union GMB gave just £290,125 in that quarter.[38]

Labour's annual conference in Liverpool in October 2023 included a 'business forum', for which two hundred executives and lobbyists bought tickets costing nearly £2,000 each. Starmer told them: 'If we do come into government, you will be coming into government with us.' He attended a reception held by London Labour that was sponsored by Zilch, a company offering 'Buy Now Pay Later' payment plans of the sort that Labour was reportedly planning to regulate.[39] Sponsors of other events included Boeing, Deliveroo and Goldman Sachs. The journalist Michael Crick, veteran of countless party conferences, tweeted: 'This is big story of Labour conference: the sell-out to dubious businesses. The lobbyists; fringe meeting sponsors paying to make speeches; cash for access. And sod the unions.'[40] The party said 2023 was its biggest ever year for fundraising.[41]

Tickets for Labour's 'business conference' at the Oval cricket ground in February 2024 cost at least £995 a head. They sold out within four hours, raising almost £400,000 for the party.[42] Addressing a more expensive crowd than Corbyn had ever seen, Reeves praised profit-making, and Starmer promised to work with business leaders: 'Your fingerprints are on every one of our national missions.'

He even risked reminding them of Corbyn: 'Let's cast our minds back to 2019. Let's imagine if you were invited to an event like this, a Labour business conference, before any of the changes to our party had taken place. The question is – would you go?' The crowd laughed.[43]

Tickets to 'business day' at Labour's autumn conference of 2024 sold out within twenty-four hours. Five hundred businesspeople paid £3,000 each – a price hike of more than 50 per cent in a year. One lobbyist joked to the *FT*: 'I was told that if I didn't get two tickets I'd be out of a job.'[44]

With the election nearing, lots more people wanted to throw money at Labour, and most weren't motivated by ideological kinship. NatWest funded a member of its lobbying team to work as parliamentary assistant to the shadow business secretary, Jonathan Reynolds.[45] Consultancies – especially the giants EY and PwC – donated £287,000 in staff time to Labour in the year to September 2023. That brainpower helped the party flesh out its policies. It also helped the consultancies soften the anti-consultancy impulses of the likely next government. Reeves had previously threatened to 'slash government consultancy spending' if Labour took power. Richard Murphy, a professor of accounting practice at Sheffield University, told the *FT* that consultancies, by gifting staff time, could gain 'influence, access, phone numbers'. Corbyn's Labour appeared to have taken no staff time from these firms.[46] But then Corbyn's Labour hadn't taken power either, or even seemed very interested in taking it.

★

I'm not arguing that donors have pushed an unwilling Labour towards the centre. Rather, there is a

self-reinforcing symbiosis between the political position that the donors want, what Starmer instinctively
wants, and what seems to make electoral sense.
Donors probably encouraged Labour's centrist turn,
but they aren't the driving force. The coming question, though, is: will some donors want something
more specific from Labour in power?

When I asked Lubner what he hoped to get out
of Labour, he said a lot of people around him presumed that he was buying influence. Rich Tories in
his circle were angry with him for helping Labour,
while also asking him to get the party to drop its
plans to put VAT on private schools. Meanwhile, 'left
social media' accused him of using Labour to further
his business interests (and of being an Israel apologist, an apartheid apologist, and a Nazi).

'What am I getting back from my donations?' he
asked himself. 'I have no idea what I'm getting back.'
He didn't aspire, say, to have the next MP for Steve-
nage in his pocket. 'I'm hearing time and time again
from people in the Labour Party that what I am doing
is very unusual because I'm not asking for anything.
I'm not looking for a peerage. I don't run a company
anymore so I'm not saying, "Build more roads and
break more windscreens".'

He said that if Labour won power, he wouldn't
be phoning in with requests. He granted that if they
'do a Rwanda' on migration, he might call to say, 'I'm

really, really disappointed.' Otherwise, he has said, 'I haven't really got any advice to give.'[47]

I liked Lubner. Perhaps he charmed me into naivety. But I do think it's broadly true that the handful of most committed Labour donors, people like him and Taylor and Sainsbury, are giving because they believe in Starmer's project rather than in a quest for personal financial advantage. Their gifts also help Labour to stay relatively clean: so much money is flooding in pre-election that the party has little need to take embarrassing or 'high maintenance' donations.

The problem is that if Labour gets elected on 4 July, the inevitable disillusionments of government will turn off some idealistic donors. New donors coming on board will disproportionately be self-seeking opportunists – the types who always seek to embed themselves in the governing party. Sheikhs and the oligarch-adjacent may suddenly warm to Labour. Some of the party's new donors might well be the same people who previously invested in the Conservatives. After all, Bernie Ecclestone, the Formula One mogul whose donation sparked the first big scandal of the New Labour era, had been a Tory donor. Indeed, Mohamed Amersi, the telecoms dealmaker disappointed by the Conservatives, has put out public feelers to Labour. He told Lebedev's *Independent* in 2023:

I feel that the country needs help in many places
in the North, in the East, where societies are
broken. Crime, joblessness, poverty … these are
all huge problems. So whoever is best placed and
has a strategy on how best to deal with their constituency, I'm happy to support. If a Labour MP
comes and says: 'Look, I have been an MP here
and I need money to help with my outreach, can
you help?' I will do it.[48]

It was easy for Labour to remain relatively pure in
Opposition. Once in power, a donor-friendly party
will be the target for chancers. In addition, donations
from the likes of Lubner have bulked up the party
machine, so that Labour now has far more mouths
to feed than during the Corbyn years.

It's entirely feasible that the party will suffer some
version of the corruption that engulfed the Tories.
Here is a potential foretaste: when Vaughan Gething
was running to become Welsh Labour leader in early
2024, he took a donation of £200,000 from Dauson
Environmental Group, which is owned by the convicted environmental polluter David Neal. Gething
and Neal had history together. Months before the
donation, while Gething was economy minister, one
of Dauson's subsidiaries received a loan of £400,000
from the Development Bank of Wales, which is
owned by the Welsh government. Gething had also

lobbied National Resources Wales on behalf of Neal's businesses.[49] Gething is now First Minister of Wales. He repeatedly said he never took decisions relating to Dauson. But let's hope such strange financial coincidences don't go national if Labour wins the general election.

On the upside: Labour has an incentive to staunch the flow of British political donations. Even in 2023, when the party looked to be steaming towards power, the Tories often outraised it. After Labour's record takings of £10.5 million in the second quarter, for instance, the Conservatives netted £15.4 million in the third quarter.[50] Labour will probably never become the default party for rich donors. Its long-term self-interest is to limit British election spending, and close loopholes to foreign money. But the short-term temptation in power will be to take all the dosh that will suddenly be on offer.

7

WHAT IS TO BE DONE?

The real concern should be that the UK has taken the first steps on a journey towards state capture which ends in being a mid-ranking, politically unstable semi-democracy, with a mid-level economy, in which corruption is prevalent and government is for the purpose of self-perpetuation and not the public interest.

Robert Barrington, Professor of Anti-Corruption Practice at the Centre for the Study of Corruption, University of Sussex[1]

Political parties often collapse amid a rash of scandals and as I was finishing this book the Tories came up with a cracker even by their own recent standards. At 3.15 a.m. one night in December 2023, the Conservative MP Mark Menzies rang his 78-year-old former campaign manager and asked: 'Are you on your own? I've got in with some bad people and they've got me locked in a flat and they want £5,000 to release me.' Menzies had hit a spot of bother with some male sex-workers. Now he wanted the 78-year-old to give him the money from a bank account that contained donations to his campaign, revealed Billy Kenber of *The Times*.[2]

She refused. Instead, the next morning, Menzies' constituency office manager, Shirley Green, paid up, reportedly by cashing in her own ISA savings account. Kenber, heroically keeping a straight face, reported that Menzies

> summoned one of his staffers to London to collect him from the flat. On arrival, the junior employee handed over his own money, a sum thought to be a few hundred pounds, which Menzies said he owed to two other men.
>
> Asked if he was concerned he could be black-mailed again, Menzies said he would change his phone number.

Menzies was a veteran of scandal. His record, according to *The Times*, included being accused of fighting with an acquaintance after getting that person's dog drunk. (He denied the allegation.) Still, when the article appeared, he resigned from the Conservative Party, lost his post as a government trade envoy, and said he would step down as an MP at the next election.

The accusation that ended his political career wasn't to do with sex-workers or drunk dogs. It was that Menzies had allegedly paid off the sex-workers with campaign donations. Again, he denied it. In the course of telling the story, though, *The Times* revealed yet another loophole in the UK's feeble campaign-finance laws:

> The money was in an account with the name Fylde Westminster Group and was set up as a local business group to allow supporters to donate to Menzies ... The practice of setting up a local business group is common among MPs because donors do not have to declare a donation to the Conservative Party in company accounts, and donors are not publicly declared at all until they reach a certain threshold.

The Times said Menzies had repeatedly used money from the fund for private medical expenses. It added that the Conservative Party had known about the allegations against him for more than three months, yet hadn't sanctioned him. Menzies said, 'I strongly dispute the allegations put to me. I have fully complied with all the rules for donations.'

The story completed a bizarre hattrick. Menzies' constituency was Fylde in Lancashire, just outside Blackpool. The two Tory MPs in seats adjoining his, Scott Benton and Paul Maynard, had both been hit by financial scandals within the previous twelve months. Benton was punished for offering to lobby, while Maynard used taxpayers' money for party work.

Imagine the damage all this did to public trust in Blackpool, a deprived town with England's lowest life expectancy.[3] Trust was the central issue at a hustings event held at Blackpool Cricket Club before the by-election on 2 May for Benton's seat (which Labour would win with a mind-blowing twenty-six-point swing). Reform UK's candidate, Mark Butcher, told the hustings there was 'no integrity left' in either the Labour or Tory parties. Instead of career politicians, he said, 'We need to bring people back into politics, and then integrity would be a big part of that.'[4]

Political corruption is a gift to parties like Reform. Nationally, only 12 per cent of Britons said they trusted political parties in 2024 – the lowest score for any public institution, reported the Office for National Statistics.[5] Keir Starmer said,

> Trust in politics is now so low, so degraded, that nobody believes you can make a difference anymore. After the sex scandals, the expenses scandals, the waste scandals, the contracts for friends, even in a crisis like the pandemic, people have looked at us and concluded we're all just in it for ourselves.[6]

A political system in that kind of condition needs to clean itself up, or be destroyed by Trumpian populists promising to clean it up. Sunak's Conservatives seem to have given up even trying. Tackling corruption had fallen to the bottom of their list of priorities, if such a list existed. By spring 2024, the role of anti-corruption champion in government had remained unfilled since John Penrose resigned in despair under Boris Johnson nearly two years earlier.[7] Nor had Sunak's government yet produced an official 'anti-corruption strategy' to replace the one that expired in 2022.[8] Any cleansing will be left to a new government.

What could a cleaner British political system look like? And what might be the inevitable downsides of any reform?

*

The optimal moment to cleanse politics is when public tolerance of elite corruption expires, and when a new ruling elite replaces the old one. With the general election of July 2024, the UK looks as if it's about to get there. The havoc wrought by Brexit on Britain's already blurry constitutional underpinnings adds further impetus to reform. For instance, the UK needs to find alternatives to the EU's Charter of Fundamental Rights.[9]

Labour has talked a good game about tackling corruption. It has been vague about what exactly it will do, beyond promising to set up an independent ethics and integrity commission with vast powers to investigate rule-breaking. Starmer has mooted stiffer jail sentences for offenders.[10] However, Britain's courts are already overwhelmed. And prosecutions of politicians – some of whom may have made innocent mistakes – could dissuade even more people from going into politics.

What the system probably needs instead is a concept of 'dishonourable discharge': any politician who breaks certain rules couldn't be a minister or MP again, would lose their political pension, wouldn't get an honour, and would incur a blot on their official record.

Other political systems show that cleansing is possible. Almost immediately after Emmanuel Macron became French president in 2017, his parliament passed a law on 'the moralisation of politics': no longer could MPs hire relatives, spend without providing receipts, or moonlight as consultants. The most prominent victim of the reforms was former French prime minister François Fillon, who had employed his Welsh wife as a fictitious parliamentary assistant. Over thirty-two years, Fillon had paid her more than €1 million in state funds for work she didn't do.

This had long been normal behaviour in Paris. Lots of politicians employed spouses. Any ministers who landed in legal trouble were judged by a court of their peers, who tended to the view, 'There, but for the grace of God ...' But under Macron the age of leniency was over. Fillon was sentenced to four years in prison, three of them suspended. The president he had served, Nicolas Sarkozy, was sentenced to a year's imprisonment for illegal financing of his failed bid for re-election in 2012. In 2024 the legal cases were still ongoing, and neither man had yet spent a day in prison. Still, by French standards, this was an end to elite shamelessness.[11]

China under President Xi Jinping went about cleansing in its own way. A paper by three Chinese economists in 2024, titled 'A "Leaner" Government?',[12] described a traditional form of Chinese corruption:

Extravagant dining and wining with public funds was prevalent in government, public institutions, and SOEs [state-owned enterprises] across the country. Chinese officials have long held lavish liquor-drenched receptions for visiting colleagues and business elites, where baijiu ('white spirit' by literal translation) plays a very important role in political networking and business brokerage. Similarly, entrepreneurs usually throw lavish banquets for officials to obtain economic gains from favorable treatment by the government (i.e., rent-seeking). Moreover, the expensive high-end baijiu itself is an ideal 'bribe currency' in China.

After Xi became president in 2012, he launched a

crackdown on corruption. Banquets went out of vogue. The result, report the economists: the average body-mass index and probability of being overweight fell for public-sector employees. The anti-corruption drive seemed to be working.

Britain's next government will need to roll out its own version of 'moralisation of politics'. The task is to turn the defunct norms of the Good Chaps 'state of mind' into 'cold hard prose', write Andrew Blick and Peter Hennessy.[13] The UK needs a system that can work even when staffed by Bad Chaps. That means replacing a moral code of behaviour with written rules. To some degree, this has been happening gradually since the cash-for-questions scandal of the 1990s, or even before.[14] The MPs' expenses scandal of 2009 prompted another burst of rule-writing. In particular, MPs now have to produce receipts for every penny they spend, and get them approved by their new watchdog, the Independent Parliamentary Standards Authority.

All over Westminster, elected politicians will increasingly be placed under the oversight of unelected watchdogs. (We'll also need to keep a watch on the watchdogs themselves. They too can slip the leash. John Bourn, a ferocious money-saving Auditor-General for two decades until 2008, turned out to have spent £365,000 in three years on dozens of questionably useful foreign trips with his wife and secretary, including first-class flights and five-star hotels.)[15]

I promise not to draw up minute blueprints of what reform of the British system should look like. Many parliamentary committees and experts have already done so. Readers looking for blueprints should consult recent books such as *Downward Spiral* by John Bowers and *Bonfire of the Decencies* by Andrew Blick and Peter Hennessy, as well as reports by Transparency International,[16] by the MP Margaret Hodge,[17] and by the UK Governance Project chaired by Dominic Grieve.[18]

But the general direction of travel seems clear. There will be stricter rules on political donations, the outsourcing of government work, the awarding of honours and ministers' behaviour. No longer should the prime minister have a hand in choosing the heads of watchdogs, from their own ethics adviser to the BBC. The PM can control the executive, but not the people who check on the executive.

Another sensible reform looks, sadly, unfeasible: banning political donations and replacing them with proper state funding for political parties. That could be done for about £150 million a year, or just over £2 per Briton. It would probably save money in the long run, partly by removing the incentive for politicians to funnel public money to party donors, as in the Covid VIP lane scandal. But with so few Britons now trusting political parties, it would be a tricky law to pass. Just imagine the *Daily Mail*'s front page.

Whatever form the reforms take, they will cage Britain's political elite inside an unprecedentedly rules-based system. As the historian Tacitus wrote, 'The more corrupt the state, the more numerous its laws.'[19] British government will get numerous laws. In many ways, this will suck. More checks will mean more bureaucracy: more boring forms to fill in, more civil servants to scrutinise them, more quangos and quangocrats. All this will offend against the traditional spirit of the British government, which is that elected politicians outrank 'unelected bureaucrats'.

Cumbersome rules will also slow down government. The Whitehall of the near future won't look like the nimble Silicon Valley start-up of Dominic Cummings' imagination. Then, as Tacitus noted, any reforms will leave loopholes that people will exploit.[20] There will be all sorts of other unintended consequences that will require unpicking. And in the short run, tighter rules will mean more people get caught, meaning more scandals, and potentially more damage to public trust.

But there is an eternal pendulum swing in any system between underregulation and overregulation. British government is about to jump from under- to overregulation. Then, over the years, it will find ways to relax the overregulation. The harbinger is what has happened in the Commons: the parliamentary watchdog IPSA has gradually been able to relax its initial overregulation of MPs' financial matters.

IPSA started life in 2010 very tough and suspicious. Over time, as fraudulent expenses became rare, it tried to loosen up. Even the most sanctimonious regulator doesn't want to spend its days arguing over sandwich purchases. IPSA's then chair Ruth Evans told a parliamentary committee in 2017:[21]

> We judged that it is time now, some years since the expenses scandal, for us to be able to entrust MPs with a greater degree of discretion over the way they use their budgets … We recognise the distinctive demands on MPs in a way that we haven't before – recognising that they work in two locations and have very demanding workloads, and that that needs to be compatible with family life … we are some way down the line from those early days of IPSA, when we were established in the light of an expenses scandal.

Evans said she wanted to treat MPs 'as grown-ups in charge of their own budgets, and not penny-pinch and second-guess all the time'. IPSA's chief executive, Marcial Boo, cited the example of hotel stays. An MP's permitted budget for one night in a London hotel at the time was £150. Boo explained:

It was the case, from time to time, that an MP would stay three nights in London, and because hotels vary their rates, one of those night may have been £170, even though another night might be under £150. The rules of our scheme, because we were applying them faithfully, meant that we needed to recover that extra £20. We have now allowed more flexibility, so that, so long as the average of the hotel stays is under £150, it doesn't matter whether a particular night is a little bit more.

As the rules on MPs' expenses bedded in, and came to be taken for granted by most people on both sides, there has been a swing from hypervigilance to a more principles-based regulation. The rules for expenses that were written after the 2009 scandal have slowly turned into taken-for-granted norms. No MP still expects the taxpayer to buy them a duckhouse.

I suspect that over time, the same will happen with stricter rules imposed across Westminster and Whitehall. Officials will no longer expect to be able to jump straight from government to lobbying. Ministers won't expect to throw contracts to donors. Prime ministers won't expect to save ministers who do. The red tape will gradually start to become invisible, rather than feeling like a daily obstacle. New political norms will grow. There are ways to encourage this growth, for instance by introducing the 'dishonour-able discharge', or making ministers swear oaths of office.

I got a glimpse of what a system with cleaner norms looks like when talking to a friend of mine who had been a cabinet minister in Sweden. A businessman had offered to take him by private jet to see the England–Sweden game at the football World Cup of 2006. My friend, a big football fan, was sorely tempted. But he understood that it was unthink-able to say yes. If the story came out, he'd be sunk. Swedish voters wouldn't accept a politician going on a jolly paid for by a businessperson. My friend didn't have to check the written rules. He just knew that the offer didn't meet what John Major calls the 'smell test'.[22]

The British political system during the 'Good Chaps' era rested on unspoken norms of this kind. As those norms faded, especially from the early 1990s, bad behaviour spiked. Now we're going to enter an era of written rules. When we come out of it, we may start breeding more Good Chaps again.

NOTES

A Word in Advance

1   BBC News, 'UK is not a corrupt country, says Boris Johnson', 10 November 2021.
2   United Nations Office on Drugs and Crime, 'Corruption: a baseline definition', undated.

1. Life and Death of the Good Chap

1   In *The Strand Magazine*, volume 85, 1933, p. 6, retrieved at https://www.google.fr/books/edition/The_Strand_Magazine/9.
2   Clive Priestley, 'Promoting the Efficiency of Central Government', in Arthur Shenfield et al., *Managing the Bureaucracy* (Adam Smith Institute, London, 1986), p. 117.
3   Peter Hennessy, 'Harvesting the Cupboards': Why Britain Has Produced No Administrative Theory or Ideology in the Twentieth Century (Transactions of the Royal Historical Society, Vol. 4 (1994), p. 205.
4   Ibid., p. 205
5   Ibid., p. 205.
6   *The Economist*, 'Goodbye, good chap', 18 December 2018.
7   Andrew Blick and Peter Hennessy, *The Bonfire of the Decencies: Repairing and Restoring the British Constitution* (Haus Publishing, London, 2022), p. 139.
8   Margaret Hodge, *Losing our moral compass: Corrupt*

money and corrupt politics (APPG on Anti-Corruption &
Responsible Tax, June 2023), pp. 83–4.

9   Transparency International, 'Concerns of corruption at
all-time high as UK falls to its lowest ever score on global
Corruption Perceptions Index', 30 January 2024.

10 Hodge, *Losing our moral compass,* p. 7.

11 Rory Stewart, *Politics On the Edge: A Memoir from Within*
(Jonathan Cape, London, 2023), p. 26.

12 Leslie Holmes, *Corruption: A Very Short Introduction*
(Oxford University Press, Oxford, 2015), pp. 59–60.

13 John Bowers, *Downward Spiral: Collapsing public standards
and how to restore them* (Manchester University Press,
Manchester, 2024), p. 209.

14 David Kynaston, 'Obituary: John Profumo', *Financial
Times,* 10 March 2006.

15 Andrew Roth, 'Obituary: John Profumo', *Guardian,* 10
March 2006 and Matthew Parris, *Great Parliamentary
Scandals: Four Centuries of Calumny, Smear & Innuendo*
(Robson Books, London, 1997), pp. 153–78.

16 Churchill Archives Centre, '"Marples Must Go!" The
controversial life and career of Ernest Marples', undated;
Telegraph, 'Reginald Ridgway', 29 March 2002; and
Lewis Baston, 'Ernest Marples. Yes, a rogue – but he
brightened up the 1950s, and he made things happen',
Conservative Home, 7 March 2014.

17 Parris, *Great Parliamentary Scandals,* pp. 178–84.

18 Oliver Bullough, *Moneyland: Why Thieves & Crooks Now
Rule the World & How to Take it Back* (Profile Books,
London, 2018), pp. 32–3.

19 TaxPayers' Alliance, 'Income tax', 18 January 2023,
retrieved at https://www.taxpayersalliance.com/
income_tax_briefing retrieved on 10 January 2024.

20 Bowers, *Downward Spiral,* p. 31.

21   David Hencke, 'Tory MPs were paid to plant questions
     says Harrods chief', *Guardian*, 20 October 1994.
22   Blick and Hennessy, *The Bonfire of the Decencies*, p. 15.
23   Bowers, *Downward Spiral*, p. 7.
24   Peter Riddell, 'Ministers also have rights – balancing
     executive prerogatives and executive scrutiny',
     Inaugural Public Lecture at University College London,
     26 April 2023, retrieved at https://www.ucl.ac.uk/
     constitution-unit/sites/constitution_unit/files/peter_
     riddell_inaugural_lecture.pdf

2. Shameless

1   Tweet by Stefan Dercon on 25 January 2024,
     retrieved at https://x.com/gamblingondev/
     status/1750598575279493476 on 7 May 2024.
2   Ian Buruma, *The Missionary and the Libertine: Love and War
     in East and West* (Faber and Faber, London, 1996), p. 92.
3   Clare Garner, 'Referendum candidate gives way to Clark',
     Independent, 29 January 1997.
4   Tom Burgis, '"Can I now send the funds?": secrets of the
     Conservative money machine', *Guardian*, 27 February
     2024.
5   Sue Gaisford, 'Behind Closed Doors – London's dens of
     iniquity', *Financial Times*, 15 August 2022.
6   Jackie Daly, 'The secrets of Robin Birley's new
     homewares collection', *Financial Times*, 4 February 2022.
7   Nadine Dorries, *The Plot: The Political Assassination of
     Boris Johnson* (HarperCollins, London, 2023), p. 45.
8   Jan-Werner Müller, 'Trump, Johnson and the real
     problem with populism', *Financial Times*, 17 June 2023.
9   *The Economist*, 'Looters with flags', 2 September 2023.
10   Lucy Fisher, Rafe Uddin and Anna Gross, 'Scale of

misconduct by MPs "undermines trust" in Westminster',
Financial Times, 16 December 2023.

11 Randeep Ramesh, 'Grant Shapps admits he had second
job as "millionaire web marketer" while MP', *Guardian*, 15
March 2015 and Emma Loffhagen, 'Meet Grant Shapp's,
the UK's new defence secretary', *Evening Standard*, 31
August 2023.

12 Jessica Murray, 'Lawyers raise alarm at struggle to tackle
UK local government corruption', *Guardian*, 2 February
2024.

13 Holmes, *Corruption*, p. 45.

14 Robert Barrington, 'There is more corruption and
corruption risk in and around this government than any
British government since 1945', LSE British Politics and
Policy, 25 November 2021.

15 IPPR, 'Revealed: trust in politicians at lowest level on
record', 5 December 2021, retrieved at https://www.ippr.
org/news-and-media/press-releases/revealed-trust-in-
politicians-at-lowest-level-on-record/ on 10 January 2024.

16 Adam Bienkov, 'Just One Per Cent of Voters Say
Rishi Sunak's Government is "Very Honest"', *Byline
Times*, 5 January 2024, retrieved at https://bylinetimes.
com/2024/01/05/just-one-per-cent-of-voters-say-rishi-
sunaks-government-is-very-honest/ on 10 January 2024.

17 See, among many others, Ipsos, 'Trust in politicians
reaches its lowest score in 40 years', 14 December 2023;
Christopher McKeon, 'Trust in government hits record
low as 75% polled say UK is heading wrong way',
Independent, 28 February 2023; and King's College London
News Centre, 'UK has internationally low confidence in
political institutions, police and press', 30 March 2023.

18 Tom Bower, *Broken Vows: Tony Blair, The Tragedy of Power*
(Faber & Faber, London, 2016), pp. 486–8 and p. 496.

19 Hodge, *Losing our moral compass*, p. 79.

20 Ibid., p. 6.

21 Sam Knight, 'What have fourteen years of Conservative rule done to Britain?', *New Yorker*, 25 March 2024.

22 Vikram Dodd, 'Recorded crime in England and Wales at 20-year high as charge rate hits new low', *Guardian*, 21 July 2022 retrieved at https://www.theguardian.com/uk-news/2022/jul/21/recorded-in-england-and-wales-at-20-year-high-as-charge-rate-hits-new-low on 10 January 2024.

3. The Donors Have Spoken

1 See Best for Britain's tweet on 6 June 2022 at https://x.com/BestForBritain/status/1533818598086541312?s=20

2 See Rebecca Davis O'Brien and Nicholas Nehamas, 'How Much Cash Did Ron DeSantis Burn Through Against Trump?', 1 February 2024; and Sam Freedman's tweet on 3 February 2024 at https://x.com/Samfr/status/1753764513894093200?s=20.

3 *McCartney: A Life in Lyrics*, Season 2, Episode 11, 'Michelle' after 17.30 minutes, podcast series.

4 UK Parliament, 'Partied out: Political party membership', undated.

5 Gordon Cramb, 'Lord McAlpine: Tory fundraiser and Thatcher's loyal confidant', *Financial Times*, 19 January 2014.

6 Roland Gribben, 'Nadir seeks SFO deal in bid to return home. Fraud office will not be drawn but advisers say exile wants bail agreement', *Telegraph*, 3 September 2003.

7 Jim Pickard, 'Lord McAlpine urges return of Nadir money', *Financial Times*, 24 August 2012.

8 Bowers, *Downward Spiral*, p. 17.

9 Rachel Stevenson and agencies, 'Blair intervened over F1

tobacco ban exemption, documents show', *Guardian*, 12 October 2008.

10 Hodge, *Losing our moral compass*, p. 53.

11 Committee on Standards in Public Life, 'Political party finance: ending the big donor culture', November 2011, p. 21.

12 Ibid., p. 35.

13 Julia Cagé, *Le prix de la démocratie* (Gallimard, Paris, 2022), p. 182.

14 Committee on Standards in Public Life, 'Political party finance', p. 60.

15 Daniel Chandler, 'Big money is trashing trust in British politics. "Democracy vouchers" could be the solution', *Guardian*, 29 August 2023.

16 Committee on Standards in Public Life, 'Political party finance', p. 9.

17 Bowers, *Downward Spiral*, p. 117.

18 Committee on Standards in Public Life, 'Political party finance', p. 25.

19 ITV News, 'David Cameron on political campaigns', 27 September 2012.

20 Andrew Edgecliffe-Johnson, 'Cameron fluffs his lines on Letterman test', *Financial Times*, 27 September 2012.

21 Cagé, *Le prix de la démocratie*, pp. 84–5 and p. 92.

22 Tim Bale, *The Conservative Party after Brexit: Turmoil and Transformation* (Polity Press, Cambridge, 2023), p. 4.

23 BBC News, 'Party spending on 2010 general election falls by £10m', 2 December 2010.

24 Chandler, 'Big money is trashing trust in British politics', *Guardian*.

25 Nick Mathiason and Yuba Bessaoud, 'Tory Party Funding from City Doubles under Cameron', The Bureau of Investigative Journalism, 8 February 2011.

26   LSE Event, 'Money and Politics: analysing donations to UK political parties, 2000–2021', 25 January 2023, after 1:27:19 hours, viewed at https://www.youtube.com/watch?v=FJX_spi6Asc&list=PLK4elntcUEy2eonA4OlH9GkBGVFC6fNwe&index=11,

27   Stuart Wilks-Heeg, 'Who pays for the party, and why?', Centre for Crime and Justice Studies, December 2013.

28   Peter Geoghegan, *Democracy For Sale: Dark Money and Dirty Politics* (Head of Zeus, London, 2021), p. 144.

29   Daniel Boffey and Haroon Siddique, 'Tory treasurer's cash-for-access boast unacceptable, says David Cameron', *Guardian*, 25 March 2012.

30   Mirko Draca, Colin Green and Swarnodeep Homroy, 'Financing UK democracy: A stocktake of 20 years of political donations', CAGE working paper no. 642, November 2022, p. 7 and pp. 17–19.

31   LSE Event, 'Money and Politics'; see video at 35.30 minutes.

32   Draca, Green and Homroy, 'Financing UK democracy', CAGE working paper.

33   'Lord Michael Farmer' at https://www.lordmichaelfarmer.co.uk .

34   LSE Event, 'Money and Politics'.

35   Dominic Kennedy and Oliver Moody, 'Peter Virdee: Tories and Labour kept taking dirty cash from fraud tycoon', *The Times*, 23 March 2022, and *Der Spiegel*, 'Batman' zu mehr als drei Jahren Haft verurteilt', 23 December 2021.

36   Cynthia O'Murchu, Stefania Palma and Jasmine Cameron-Chileshe, 'Tory donor charged in Puerto Rico bribery scheme', *Financial Times*, 5 August 2022.

37   Alex Figueroa Cancel, 'FBI contó con 27 informantes en

el caso contra Wanda Vázquez, Julio Herrera Velutini y Mark Rossini', *El Nuevo Día*, 23 January 2024.

38 Andrew Sparrow, 'No. 10 chief of staff spoken to by FBI about work for banker accused of bribery', *Guardian*, 18 September 2022.

39 Tweet by Heidi Blake of the *New Yorker* at https://x.com/HeidilBlake/status/1717943469375713348?s=20 on 27 October 2023.

40 Heidi Blake, Tom Warren, Richard Holmes and Jane Bradley, 'The UK Refused To Raid A Company Suspected Of Money Laundering, Citing Its Tory Donations', *Buzzfeed News*, 19 April 2018.

41 Tweet by Heidi Blake of the *New Yorker* at https://x.com/HeidilBlake/status/1717943007821865086?s=20 on 27 October 2023.

42 Jasper Jolly, 'JCB built and supplied equipment to Russia months after saying exports had stopped', *Guardian*, 15 May 2024.

43 Anna Isaac, 'HMRC investigating tax affairs of one of Tory party's largest donors', *Guardian*, 27 September 2023.

44 Ben Stupples, 'Billionaire Tory Donor Sees Fortune Boom Amid Reported Tax Probe', Bloomberg News, 11 October 2023.

45 LSE Event, 'Money and Politics', see video at 38.20 minutes.

46 Bale, *The Conservative Party after Brexit,* p. 191.

47 Peter Geoghegan, Seth Thévoz and Jenna Corderoy, 'Revealed: The elite dining club behind £130m+ donations to the Tories', *Open Democracy*, 22 November 2019.

48 Jasmine Cameron-Chileshe and Laurence Fletcher, 'Billionaire Tory donor Michael Hintze nominated for life peerage', *Financial Times*, 14 October 2022.

49   Rupert Neate, 'Tory donor's £82m earnings surpass hedge fund rivals in difficult year', *Guardian*, 11 January 2023.

50   Andrew Graystone, 'The Marshall Plan', *Prospect*, 27 March 2024.

51   Tim Shipman, *All Out War: The Full Story of Brexit* (William Collins, London, 2017), p. 169 and p. 576.

52   Graystone, 'The Marshall Plan', *Prospect*.

53   Gregory Davis, 'Revealed: The Shocking Tweets of GB News Co-owner Sir Paul Marshall', Hopenothate.org, 22 February 2024.

54   Graystone, 'The Marshall Plan', *Prospect*.

55   Davis, 'Revealed', Hopenothate.org.

56   Daniel Thomas and Harriet Agnew, 'Paul Marshall, the financier turned media baron bankrolling GB News', *Financial Times*, 9 March 2024.

57   Harriet Agnew and Daniel Thomas, 'Paul Marshall, the hedge fund boss readying a bid for the *Telegraph*', *Financial Times*, 16 October 2023.

58   Christopher McKeon and Anthony France, '"Hypocrite" Tory who hit out at MPs needing extra salary gets £100,000 for GB News job', *Evening Standard*, 22 March 2023.

59   Anna Wise, 'GB News investor Sir Paul Marshall steps down from board', *Independent*, 26 April 2024.

60   The Conversation, 'Fact Check: do 89% of businesses really support Remain?', 14 June 2016.

61   Libby Watson, 'US financial firms spent almost $3 million against "Brexit"', Sunlight Foundation, 22 June 2016.

62   Caroline Mortimer, 'Brexit campaign was largely funded by five of UK's richest businessmen', *Independent*, 24 April 2017.

63   Henry Mance, 'Brexit donors guided by bitter experience with EU', *Financial Times*, 15 June 2016.

64   Ibid.

65   Frances Coppola, 'Britain: The Tories aren't the Party of Business – just the London Financial Elite', Open Democracy, 27 November 2019.

66   Shipman, *All Out War*, p. 406.

67   Paul Dallison, 'Murdoch newspapers registered as official Leave campaigners', *Politico*, 29 November 2016.

68   Geoghegan, *Democracy For Sale*, p. 145.

69   Ben Chapman, 'Brexit-backing hedge fund billionaire Crispin Odey suffers record losses as UK stock market surges to all-time high', *Independent*, 6 January 2017.

70   Nadeem Badshah, 'Brexit donors furious at high tax bills', *The Times*, 23 December 2017.

71   Geoghegan, *Democracy For Sale*, pp. 70–83.

72   Peter Geoghegan and Jenna Corderoy, '"Not in the public interest": why the Electoral Commission didn't investigate Vote Leave and DUP donation', Open Democracy, 1 April 2019.

73   Geoghegan, *Democracy For Sale*, p. 118.

74   John Johnston, 'Britain's political parties are quietly raking in millions. No one will say where it's coming from', *Politico.eu*, 8 June 2023.

75   Electoral Commission, 'Vote Leave fined and referred to the police for breaking electoral law', 17 July 2018.

76   Jolyon Maugham, *Bringing Down Goliath* (WH Allen, London, 2023), p. 149.

77   Donatienne Ruy, 'Did Russia Influence Brexit?', Centre for Strategic & International Studies, 21 July 2020.

78   Geoghegan, *Democracy For Sale*, p. 30.

79   Jim Pickard and Camilla Hodgson, 'Vote Leave fined and referred to police', *Financial Times*, 17 July 2018.

80 Geoghegan and Corderoy, 'Not in the public interest'.

81 Committee on Standards in Public Life, 'Political party finance', p. 23.

82 Katy Scott, 'Peter Murrell charged with embezzlement in SNP finance probe', BBC, 18 April 2024.

83 Rest is Politics podcast, 'From Putin to peerages', 3 April 2024, after 6.30 minutes.

84 Geoghegan, Thévoz and Corderoy, 'Revealed: The elite dining club behind £130m+ donations to the Tories', Open Democracy.

85 LSE Event, 'Money and Politics', after 1:25:36 hours.

86 Jess Garland, 'Deal or No Deal: How to put an end to party funding scandals', Electoral Reform Society, February 2015, pp. 7–8.

87 Bale, *The Conservative Party after Brexit,* pp. 59–60.

88 Geoghegan, *Democracy For Sale,* p. 145.

89 Ibid., p. 234.

90 University of Warwick, Department of Economics, 'Almost half of UK political donations come from private wealthy "super-donors", new research finds', 23 November 2022.

91 Will Dunn, 'Christopher Harborne: the silent donor behind Brexit and Boris Johnson', *New Statesman,* 18 January 2023.

92 Anna Isaac, 'Who is Anthony Bamford, the billionaire "super-donor"?', *Guardian,* 27 September 2023.

93 Isaac, 'HMRC investigating tax affairs of one of Tory party's largest donors', *Guardian.*

94 Geoghegan, *Democracy For Sale,* p. 302.

95 Charlotte Edwardes, 'Our man in Westminster: *Tatler* asks, who is the newly knighted entrepreneur, society fixer and former Tory co-chair Sir Ben Elliot?', *Tatler,* February 2021.

96 Tabby Kinder and Daniel Thomas, 'Quintessentially concierge service set up escort agency's website', *Financial Times*, 27 November 2020.

97 Jamie Nimmo and Sabah Meddings, 'Friends in high places, but is Quintessentially really worth £140m?', *Sunday Times*, 16 January 2022.

98 George Parker, Sebastian Payne, Tom Burgis, Kadhim Shubber, Jim Pickard and Jasmine Cameron-Chileshe, 'Inside Boris Johnson's Money Network', *Financial Times*, 30 July 2021.

99 Burgis, '"Can I now send the funds?": secrets of the Conservative money machine', *Guardian*.

100 Kinder and Thomas, 'Quintessentially concierge service set up escort agency's website', *Financial Times*.

101 Jessica Elgot, 'Tory chair Ben Elliot resigns after Liz Truss announced as leader', *Guardian*, 5 September 2022.

102 Jim Pickard, Tabby Kinder and Daniel Thomas, 'Boris Johnson under pressure to sack Tory fundraiser over Russia links', *Financial Times*, 3 March 2022; and Tom Burgis, *Cuckooland : Where the Rich Own the Truth* (William Collins, London, 2024), pp. 45–6.

103 Jane Merrick, 'Questions in Parliament over £1.4m government contract with Tory chairman's firm Quintessentially' inews.co.uk, 13 July 2020.

104 Edwardes, 'Our man in Westminster', *Tatler*.

105 Parker et al., 'Inside Boris Johnson's Money Network', *Financial Times*.

106 Anoosh Chakelian, 'Zac talks to Politics Home Magazine,' ZacGoldsmith.com, 17 October 2019.

107 The Editorial Board, 'The Conservatives and the whiff of chumocracy', *Financial Times*, 1 August 2021.

108 Parker et al., 'Inside Boris Johnson's Money Network', *Financial Times*.

109 Gabriel Pogrund and Henry Zeffman, 'A dinner with Charles, then the begging letter arrived', *Sunday Times*, 1 August 2021.

110 Burgis, *Cuckooland,* p. 76 and p. 147.

111 Burgis, '"Can I now send the funds?": secrets of the Conservative money machine', *Guardian.*

112 Ibid.

113 Burgis, *Cuckooland,* p. 157.

114 Parker et al., 'Inside Boris Johnson's Money Network', *Financial Times.*

115 Edwardes, 'Our man in Westminster', *Tatler.*

116 Parker et al., 'Inside Boris Johnson's Money Network', *Financial Times.*

117 BBC Verify Team, 'Budget 2024: Is the tax take the highest for 70 years?', BBC News, 6 March 2024.

118 The Editorial Board, 'The Conservatives and the whiff of chumocracy', *Financial Times.*

119 Nicole I. Guler, 'UK planning reforms: Looking back on 2021 and forward to 2022', Urbanist Architecture, 7 December 2021; and Sebastian Payne, 'Boris Johnson targets shake-up of English planning system', *Financial Times*, 2 August 2020.

120 Geoghegan, *Democracy For Sale,* p. 317.

121 Burgis, *Cuckooland,* p. 157 and p. 196.

122 Stephen Ansolabehere, John M. de Figueiredo & James M. Snyder, 'Why Is There So Little Money in Politics', National Bureau of Economic Research, January 2003.

123 Gabriel Pogrund, Emanuele Midolo, Tom Calver and George Greenwood, 'He saw my video, he got the gist', *Sunday Times*, 21 June 2020; and Jim Pickard, 'Jenrick authorised property scheme after lobbying', *Financial Times*, 31 May 2020.

124 Diversity UK, 'Lord Nash appointed as Government's lead NED', 31 July 2020.

125 Will Dunn, 'Revealed: the Tory peer linked to £3.8bn in government contracts', *New Statesman*, 23 February 2024.

126 Bowers, *Downward Spiral*, p. 72.

127 Robert Shrimsley, 'Conservatives and the sorry state of public patronage', *Financial Times*, 22 February 2023.

128 Bowers, *Downward Spiral*, p. 72.

129 Ibid., p. 229.

130 Aubrey Allegretti and Jim Waterson, 'Paul Dacre pulls out of running to be next Ofcom chair', *Guardian*, 20 November 2021.

131 Bale, *The Conservative Party after Brexit*, p. 255.

132 Gaisford, 'Behind Closed Doors – London's dens of iniquity', *Financial Times*.

133 Ben Riley-Smith and Maighna Nanu, 'Rishi Sunak stays silent as Cabinet ministers back Boris Johnson in Tories' "Operation Save Big Dog"', *Telegraph*, 16 January 2022.

134 Rupert Neate, 'Finance, property and mining: the money behind Sunak's £460,000 leadership bid', *Guardian*, 29 October 2022.

135 Elgot, 'Tory chair Ben Elliot resigns after Liz Truss announced as leader', *Guardian*.

136 Burgis, *Cuckooland*, p. 233.

137 Steven Swinford and David Brown, 'Kwasi Kwarteng's ex-boss bet big on falling pound weeks after lunch with him', *The Times*, 30 September 2022.

138 See tweet by Harry Yorke of the *Sunday Times* at https://x.com/HarryYorke1/status/1753054716911616062?s=20

139 Bowers, *Downward Spiral*, p. 117.

140 Rafe Uddin and Antonia Cundy, 'Reform UK accepted

donations from Crispin Odey despite sexual assault allegations', *Financial Times*, 1 February 2024.

141 Adam Barnett, 'Nigel Farage's Reform Party Took £135,000 from Climate Science Deniers and Fossil Fuel Interests', DeSmog, 17 November 2023.

142 Adam Barnett, Phoebe Cook and Michaela Herrmann, 'Aviation Tycoon Paid for Anti-Net Zero MP's Tory Gala Ticket', DeSmog, 20 July 2022.

143 Seth Thévoz, 'Revealed: Brexit donor behind net-zero backlash has $130m in fossil fuels', Open Democracy, 22 March 2022.

144 Tom Belger, 'Tories rake in almost five times more than Labour in recent donations', Labour List, 7 December 2023.

145 The Electoral Commission, 'Electoral Commission publishes concluded investigation update', 16 April 2024.

146 Pickard, 'Sainsbury lords become biggest donors to Tories and Labour', *Financial Times*.

147 Ben Riley-Smith, 'Health tech boss becomes biggest ever Tory donor with second £5m gift', *Daily Telegraph*, 29 February 2024.

148 Rowena Mason, Matthew Weaver and Henry Dyer, 'Biggest Tory donor said looking at Diane Abbott makes you "want to hate all black women"', *Guardian*, 11 March 2024.

149 Catherine Neilan, 'Exclusive: Tory party "sitting on" further £5m from disgraced donor Frank Hester', *Tortoise Media*, 14 March 2024.

150 EJ Ward, 'Biggest Tory donor "not racist", but was right to apologise for comments that "sound racist" Conservative peer tells LBC', LBC, 12 March 2024.

Notes

4. Russian Pioneers

1   Owen Matthews, '"It wasn't the Russian people who poisoned Skripal, it was just a few guys": Alexander Lebedev interviewed', *Spectator*, 5 October 2019.

2   David Hall, 'Privatisation, multinationals and corruption', Public Services International Research Unit, University of Greenwich, July 1999.

3   Wickham, 'Rory Stewart's Tory Leadership Campaign Is Being Bankrolled By A Russian Hedge Fund Manager', *Buzzfeed News*.

4   Sam Bright, 'Wife of Arms Deal Broker Donates £300,000 to Conservatives', *Byline Times*, 3 March 2022.

5   Alex Barker, 'Outside Edge: You are spoiling us, Sir Alan', *Financial Times*, 6 August 2010.

6   Richard Wilson, '23. British journalism's greatest ever scoops: Jonathan of Arabia (*World in Action*, David Leigh, 1995)', *Press Gazette*, 12 October 2012.

7   David Pegg and Rob Evans, 'Al-Yamamah arms deal report comes to light ending anti-corruption campaigners' battle', *Guardian*, 24 March 2024.

8   See Arthur Snell, *How Britain Broke the World: War, Greed and Blunders from Kosovo to Afghanistan, 1997–2022* (Canbury Press, Kingston upon Thames, 2022), pp. 266–7; Holmes, *Corruption*, pp. 84–5; and Ben Russell and Nigel Morris, 'Court condemns Blair for halting Saudi arms inquiry', *Independent*, 11 April 2008.

9   D. Clark, 'Number of investor visas issued to Russians in the UK 2008–2022', Statista, 11 May 2023.

10   Intelligence and Security Committee of Parliament, 'Russia', July 21, 2020, pp. 20–21.

11   Simon Kuper, 'Who are the Londoners enabling the Russian elite?', *Financial Times*, 3 March 2022.

12   Hodge, *Losing our moral compass*, p. 31.

13   Jim Pickard and Joe Miller, 'Links between Peter
     Mandelson and Jeffrey Epstein detailed in JP Morgan
     report', *Financial Times*, 21 June 2023; and Jim Pickard,
     'Mandelson met Gaddafi's son', *Financial Times*, 17 August
     2009.

14   John Heathershaw, Alexander Cooley, Tom Mayne,
     Casey Michel, Tena Prelec, Jason Sharman and Ricardo
     Soares de Oliveira, 'The UK's kleptocracy problem:
     How servicing post-Soviet elites weakens the rule of
     law', Chatham House, Russia and Eurasia Programme,
     December 2021, pp. 15–16 and p. 30.

15   Simon Kuper, 'Lunch with the *FT*: Goga Ashkenazi',
     Financial Times, 21 June 2013.

16   Gabriel Pogrund, Charles Keidan and Katherine Faulkner,
     'Charles accepted €1m cash in suitcase from sheikh',
     Sunday Times, 26 June 2022.

17   Jonathan Calvert, George Arbuthnott and Tom Calver, 'A
     prince for hire', *Sunday Times*, 9 May 2021.

18   BBC News, 'Eton boys given private audience with
     Vladimir Putin', 1 September 2016.

19   Most examples of foreign influence in the following
     paragraphs are from Simon Kuper, 'How to buy a foreign
     election', *Financial Times*, 12 February 2016.

20   Max Seddon and Michael Stothard, 'Putin awaits return
     on Le Pen investment', *Financial Times*, 4 May 2017.

21   Gavin Esler, 'Bill Browder', *Perspective*, 5 May 2022.

22   Bryant, *Code of Conduct*, pp. 99–100.

23   Jon Ungoed-Thomas, 'Russian-born husband of Tory
     donor "earned millions via oligarch connections"',
     Observer, 26 March 2022.

24   Hodge, *Losing our moral compass*, p. 55; and *Private Eye*,
     'Offshore Property: Crown jewels', 17 April 2015.

25   Annabel Sampson, 'Meet Lubov Chernukhin, whose

£1.7m makes her the biggest female Tory donor in British history', *Tatler,* 23 July 2020.

26 Robert Booth, 'Boris Johnson may pull out of tennis match with Russian ex-minister's wife', *Guardian,* 23 July 2014.

27 James Oliver, Steve Swann and Nassos Stylianou, 'Tory donor's "link" to sanctioned oligarch's secret London property', BBC News, 21 April 2022.

28 Bale, *The Conservative Party after Brexit*, p. 149.

29 Peter Geoghegan, 'Penny Mordaunt received £10,000 donation from prominent climate denier's firm', Peter Geoghegan's Substack, 17 November 2023, received by email.

30 Pickard, Kinder and Thomas, 'Boris Johnson under pressure to sack Tory fundraiser over Russia links', *Financial Times.*

31 Heathershaw et al., 'The UK's kleptocracy problem: How servicing post-Soviet elites weakens the rule of law', Chatham House, p. 41.

32 Oliver et al., 'Tory donor's "link" to sanctioned oligarch's secret London property', BBC News.

33 US Department of the Treasury, 'Treasury Sanctions Global Russian Military Supply Chain, Kremlin-linked Networks, and Elites with Western Fortunes', 14 November 2022.

34 Oliver et al., 'Tory donor's "link" to sanctioned oligarch's secret London property', BBC News.

35 Heathershaw et al., 'The UK's kleptocracy problem: How servicing post-Soviet elites weakens the rule of law', Chatham House, p. 41.

36 Oliver et al., 'Tory donor's "link" to sanctioned oligarch's secret London property', BBC News.

37 Ibid.

38   Hodge, *Losing our moral compass*, p. 58.

39   Holly Watt, 'Luxembourg-based businessman donated
      £400,000 to Tory party', *Guardian*, 25 August 2016;
      and Catherine Belton, *Putin's People: How the KGB Took
      Back Russia and* Then *Took on the West* (William Collins,
      London, 2021), p. 439.

40   Hodge, *Losing our moral compass*, p. 58.

41   Alex Wickham, 'Rory Stewart's Tory Leadership
      Campaign Is Being Bankrolled By A Russian Hedge Fund
      Manager', *Buzzfeed News*, 6 June 2019.

42   Tweet by Dmitry Leus on 8 July 2022, retrieved at
      https://x.com/DmitryLeusUK/status/
      1545350881545256962?s=20

43   Jim Fitzpatrick, 'Tory donor "reliant on Russia's FSB"
      has name removed from kleptocracy report', Open
      Democracy, 19 October 2022; and Gabriel Pogrund,
      Dipesh Gadher and Roya Nikkhah, 'The Russian banker,
      the royal fixers and a £500,000 riddle', *The Times*, 12
      September 2021.

44   Jane Bradley, 'Major Donation to UK Conservative Party
      Was Flagged Over Russia Concerns', *New York Times*, 12
      May 2022.

45   Jane Bradley, 'UK Officials Won't Investigate Political
      Donation Flagged for Russian Origins', *New York Times*,
      10 June 2022.

46   Spotlight on Corruption, 'Time to remove dirty money
      from UK political party finance', 23 March 2022.

47   George Greenwood and Sean O'Neill, 'Donations of
      £1bn trigger calls for parties to adopt corruption checks',
      The Times, 30 July 2020.

48   Bradley, 'UK Officials Won't Investigate Political
      Donation Flagged for Russian Origins', *New York Times*.

49   Oliver Bullough, *Butler to the World: How Britain Became*

the Servant of Tycoons, Tax Dodgers, Kleptocrats and
Criminals* (Profile, London, 2022), pp. 201–3.

50 Carole Cadwalladr, 'MI5 refused to investigate "Russian
spy's" links to Tories, says whistleblower', *Observer*, 21
January 2023; Dan Sabbagh and Luke Harding, 'PM
accused of cover-up over report on Russian meddling
in UK politics', *Guardian*, 4 November 2019; and Luke
Harding, 'Tory blushes deepen over activities of
Conservative Friends of Russia', *Guardian*, 30 November
2012.

51 Geoghegan, *Democracy For Sale*, p. 218.

52 Intelligence and Security Committee of Parliament,
'Russia', 21 July 2020, p. 15.

53 Ibid., p. 13.

54 Ibid., p. 12 and p. 14.

55 National Cyber Security Centre, 'UK and allies expose
Russian intelligence services for cyber campaign of
attempted political interference', 7 December 2023.

56 National Cyber Security Centre, 'Annual Review 2023', 14
November 2023, p. 23.

57 House of Commons Library, 'Research Briefing: Wilson
Doctrine'.

58 The Slow Newscast, 'Lebedev: Lord of Siberia', *Tortoise
Media*, 3 March 2022.

59 John Sweeney, 'Lebedev: The KGB Spy Who Helped Put
Putin in the Kremlin', *Byline Times*, 15 March 2022.

60 Ibid.

61 The Slow Newscast, 'Lebedev: Lord of Siberia', *Tortoise
Media*.

62 BBC News, 'Ex-KGB spy buys UK paper for £1', 21
January 2009.

63 The Slow Newscast, 'Londongrad episode 3: Project
Venus', *Tortoise Media*, 10 June 2022.

64 Stephen Brook, 'ABCs: Free London *Evening Standard* breaks through 600,000 barrier', *Guardian*, 15 January 2010.

65 Adam Bienkov, 'The Johnson-Lebedev Letters: A Back-Channel to Vladimir Putin?', *Byline Times*, 27 June 2023.

66 The Slow Newscast, 'Londongrad: The Johnson Affair', *Tortoise Media*, 14 July 2022.

67 Ibid.

68 Mark Ferguson, 'The *Evening Standard* – campaigning for Boris', Labour List, 1 May 2012.

69 Alexander Lebedev and Vladislav Inozemtsev, 'Russia and the West need a compromise over the Crimea', *Independent*, 8 November 2014.

70 Evgeny Lebedev, 'Britain must make Vladimir Putin an ally in the disaster that is Syria', *Independent*, 2 November 2015.

71 Bienkov, 'The Johnson-Lebedev Letters', *Byline Times*.

72 Matthew Weaver and Jim Waterson, 'Emily Sheffield succeeds George Osborne as *Evening Standard* editor', *Guardian*, 12 June 2020.

73 The Slow Newscast, 'Londongrad', *Tortoise Media*.

74 Pippa Crerar and Luke Harding, 'Italy "was monitoring Lebedev villa at time of Boris Johnson visit"', *Guardian*, 26 June 2023.

75 The Slow Newscast, 'Lebedev: Lord of Siberia', *Tortoise Media*.

76 The Slow Newscast, 'Londongrad', *Tortoise Media*.

77 Carole Cadwalladr, 'Boris Johnson and the Lebedevs: how I exposed the prime minister's defining scandal', *Observer*, 16 July 2022.

78 Crerar and Harding, 'Italy "was monitoring Lebedev villa at time of Boris Johnson visit"', *Guardian*.

79   Ian Cobain, 'Boris Berezovsky inquest returns open verdict on death', *Guardian,* 27 March 2014.

80   Bienkov, 'The Johnson-Lebedev Letters', *Byline Times.*

81   David Allen Green, '"As far as I am aware, no Government business was discussed" – A close reading of Boris Johnson's letter about the Lebedev meeting', the Law and Policy Blog, 26 July 2022.

82   The Slow Newscast, 'Londongrad: The Johnson Affair', *Tortoise Media.*

83   Ibid.; and tweet thread by Paul Caruana Galizia, 16 June 2022, retrieved at https://twitter.com/pcaruanagalizia/status/1537320789216833536

84   Matthews, 'Alexander Lebedev's independent mind', *Spectator.*

85   Jim Pickard, 'Boris Johnson faces fresh questions over 2018 party at Lebedev villa', *Financial Times*, 27 June 2023; and Snell, *How Britain Broke the World*, p. 196.

86   Josiah Mortimer, 'Why Did Boris Johnson Meet Evgeny Lebedev Twice in Days Before First COVID Lockdown – With No Civil Servants Present?', *Byline Times*, 30 October 2023.

87   Daniel Thomas and Jim Pickard, '*Evening Standard* takes Lebedev loans to keep afloat', *Financial Times*, 11 August 2023.

88   Mortimer, 'Why Did Boris Johnson Meet Evgeny Lebedev Twice in Days Before First COVID Lockdown – With No Civil Servants Present?', *Byline Times.*

89   Peter Jukes and Hardeep Matharu, 'Front Page Favours, Bungs and Relief: More Details Emerge of Press' Cosy COVID Relationship with Government', *Byline Times*, 1 March 2023.

90   Tweet by Dominic Cummings on 11 May 2022,

retrieved at https://twitter.com/Dominic2306/status/1524394482938093571

91   Lewis Denison, '"Possible corruption": Damaging testimony from blockbuster Covid inquiry hearing', ITV News, 31 October 2023.

92   Jukes and Matharu, 'Front Page Favours, Bungs and Relief', *Byline Times*.

93   Pickard, 'Boris Johnson faces fresh questions over 2018 party at Lebedev villa', *Financial Times*.

94   Blick and Hennessy, *The Bonfire of the Decencies*, p. 20.

95   The Slow Newscast, 'Londongrad: Lord of the Spies', *Tortoise Media*, 23 June 2022.

96   Tweet by Ian Dunt on 7 March 2024, retrieved at https://x.com/IanDunt/status/1765726088745849047?s=20

97   Evgeny Lebedev, 'I'm proud to be the first Russian lord – and I'll fight to stop online mobs killing free speech', *Mail on Sunday*, 8 August 2020.

98   Chris Bryant, *Code of Conduct: Why We Need to Fix Parliament – and How to Do It* (Bloomsbury, London, 2023), pp. 98–9; and Aubrey Allegretti, 'UK axes "golden visa" scheme after fraud and Russia concerns', *Guardian*, 17 February 2022.

99   Henry Zeffman, 'Russian link to Downing Street's new press briefing room', *The Times*, 16 March 2021.

100 Reuters, 'Russian-British businessman Lebedev pleads with Putin to end Ukraine war', 28 February 2022.

101 Jim Waterson, 'Alexander Lebedev severs links with *Independent* after Canada sanctions', *Guardian*, 24 May 2022.

102 Evgeny Lebedev, 'Russophobia is now the secret weapon of corporate hypocrites', *Evening Standard*, 28 July 2023.

103 Kate Whannel, 'What is the point of Lebedev peerage, asks ex-Lords speaker', BBC News, 9 January 2024.

104 The Good Law Project, 'Revealed: The Tories are still receiving funds from Russia-linked donors', 11 April 2023.

105 Bullough, *Butler to the World*, pp. 201–3.

5. London After Russia

1 Heba Saleh, Lucy Fisher and Emma Dunkley, 'Mohamed Mansour: the tycoon behind the Tories' biggest donation in decades', *Financial Times*, 8 June 2023.

2 Matthew Garrahan, Cynthia O'Murchu and Ahmed Al Omran, 'Hidden buyer of *Evening Standard* revealed as Saudi investor', *Financial Times*, 25 February 2019.

3 Nick Hopkins, 'Morning after: Boris Johnson recovers from Lebedev's exotic Italian party', *Guardian*, 26 July 2019.

4 Andrew Woodcock, 'Sale of stake in Independent to Saudi investor has "no influence" on editorial coverage, watchdog rules', *Independent*, 16 September 2019.

5 Peter Geoghegan, 'COP 28: Meet the top UK politicians paid big to "advise" oil rich Gulf states', Peter Geoghegan's Substack, 11 December 2023, received by email.

6 LSE Event, 'Money and Politics: analysing donations to UK political parties, 2000–2021', 25 January 2023.

7 Snell, *How Britain Broke the World*, p. 236.

8 Laura Hughes and Helen Warrell, 'MI5 warns UK MPs against "political interference" by a Chinese agent', *Financial Times*, 14 January 2022; and Steven Swinford, Fiona Hamilton and Billy Kenber, 'Revealed: China spy suspect is parliamentary aide Chris Cash', *The Times*, 11 September 2023.

9   Ben Quinn, 'Two men in UK charged with spying for China', *Guardian*, 22 April 2024.

10   Intelligence and Security Committee of Parliament, 'China', 13 July 2023, p. 2.

11   Caroline Wheeler, Dipesh Gadher, Tim Shipman and Harry Yorke, 'Commons worker arrested after allegedly spying for China', *Sunday Times*, 10 September 2023.

12   Tweet by Shen Shiwei on 13 September 2023, retrieved at https://twitter.com/shen_shiwei/status/1701949642345533860

13   Sebastian Payne, 'Labour calls on Johnson to sack Elliot as Conservative co-chair', *Financial Times*, 11 August 2021; and Tom Burgis and Andrew England, 'Tory chair failed to disclose client ties with Middle East envoys', *Financial Times*, 11 August 2021.

14   Burgis, *Cuckooland*, pp. 145–6 and p. 272.

15   Ibid., p. 146.

16   Hodge, *Losing our moral compass*, p. 4 and p. 79.

17   UK Parliament, 'Lawfare', Hansard, Volume 735, 29 June 2023.

18   Tweet by Mohamed Amersi on 18 July 2023, retrieved at https://x.com/moamersi/status/1681282843295506436?s=20

19   Tom Burgis, 'Tory donor who made fortune in Russia drops case against former MP', *Financial Times*, 27 March 2022.

20   Haroon Siddique, 'Tory donor accused of using bullying legal threats to suppress a report', *Guardian*, 3 July 2023.

21   Tweet by Amersi on 3 September 2023, retrieved at https://x.com/moamersi/status/1698254777275097231?s=20

22 Burgis, '"Can I now send the funds?": secrets of the Conservative money machine', *Guardian*

23 HP Sauce, 'A Knight's Tale: Man in the Eye', *Private Eye*, Issue 1622, 26 April – 9 May 2024.

24 Burgis, '"Can I now send the funds?": secrets of the Conservative money machine', *Guardian*.

25 Heba Saleh, Lucy Fisher and Emma Dunkley, 'Mohamed Mansour: the tycoon behind the Tories' biggest donation in decades', *Financial Times*, 8 June 2023; and Gabriel Pogrund, 'Tory treasurer chased by HMRC', *Sunday Times*, 5 February 2023.

26 Jim Pickard, 'How a start-up boss now pursued by his investors gained access to Sunak', *Financial Times*, February 29, 2024; and Jim Pickard, 'Tory donor behind Rishi Sunak private jet flight hit by £14mn asset freeze', *Financial Times*, 18 April 2024.

27 Gabriel Pogrund, 'Rishi Sunak intervenes to keep his "VIP" helicopter rides', *Sunday Times*, 17 December 2023.

28 Henry Mance, 'Rishi Sunak: ambitious pragmatist returns to take Tory leadership', *Financial Times*, 24 October 2022; and Adam Bienkov, 'Rishi Sunak's Many Failures to Fully Declare his Conflicts of Interests', *Byline Times*, 24 August 2023.

29 Ben Quinn, 'Campaigners say defeat of amendment to close loopholes on party funding leaves UK open to "malign influences"', *Guardian*, 3 May 2023; and Matei Rosca, 'UK government accused of avoiding dirty money checks on political donations despite scandals', International Consortium of Investigative Journalists, 26 June 2023.

30 Josiah Mortimer, 'UK's Next General Election is Wide Open to Foreign Interference, Corruption Watchdog Warns', *Byline Times*, 7 December 2023.

6. Labour: A Requiem for the Union Baron

1   'Same old story: Labour in hock to union paymasters –
    96 percent of donations from unions', *Daily Express,* 21
    September 2020.

2   George Parker, 'Labour party lands new megadonor in
    £5mn boost for next UK election', *Financial Times*, 4 June
    2023.

3   George Parker and Jim Pickard, 'Keir Starmer and big
    business, a love story', *Financial Times*, 15 February 2024.

4   Cagé, Le prix de la démocratie, p. 485.

5   Ibid., pp. 63–4.

6   Draca, Green and Homroy, 'Financing UK democracy',
    CAGE working paper no. 642.

7   Michael Foster, '"Why I despise Jeremy Corbyn and his
    Nazi stormtroopers", by Jewish Labour donor Michael
    Foster', *Mail on Sunday*, 14 August 2016.

8   Parker, 'Labour party lands new megadonor in £5mn
    boost for next UK election', *Financial Times.*

9   Parker and Pickard, 'Keir Starmer and big business, a love
    story', *Financial Times.*

10 Ibid.

11 Sam Harrison, 'Cambridge Chancellor donated £8
    million to EU Remain campaign', *Varsity*, 26 August 2016.

12 Eleni Courea, 'Meet the Labour think tank guiding Keir
    Starmer's path to power', *Politico,* 25 October 2023.

13 Jim Pickard, Lucy Fisher and Anna Gross, ' The think-
    tank laying the groundwork for a Labour government',
    Financial Times, 16 May 2024; and Gabriel Pogrund and
    Harry Yorke, 'The secretive guru who plotted Keir
    Starmer's path to power with undeclared cash', *Sunday
    Times*, 12 November 2023.

14 Jim Pickard, 'Labour's "mystery donor" revealed as
    hedge fund manager', *Financial Times*, 21 March 2015;

and Pickard, Fisher and Gross, 'The think-tank laying the groundwork for a Labour government', *Financial Times*.

15 Martin Taylor, 'Some Hedge Fund Managers do support the Labour Party', *Independent*, 20 March 2015.

16 Pogrund and Yorke, 'The secretive guru who plotted Keir Starmer's path to power with undeclared cash', *Sunday Times*.

17 Ibid.

18 Investigations Team, 'Labour failed to declare donations over "anti-Semitism fears"', *Telegraph,* 29 February 2024.

19 Pogrund and Yorke, 'The secretive guru who plotted Keir Starmer's path to power with undeclared cash', *Sunday Times*.

20 Harry Yorke, 'Lord Sainsbury gave biggest political donation in history to Lib Dems only to see them lose a seat', *Telegraph,* 27 February 2020.

21 Jim Pickard, 'Labour secures £2mn donation from Lord David Sainsbury', *Financial Times*, 26 February 2023.

22 Eleni Courea, 'Unite and Momentum candidates dominate Labour's selection races', *Guardian*, 5 January 2019.

23 House of Commons Library, 'General election 2019: Which party received the most donations?', 24 January 2020.

24 BBC, 'Election 2019: New leader not enough to win again, Labour warned', 19 June 2020.

25 Alix Culbertson, 'Starmer U-turns on leadership election pledge to renationalise railways', Sky News, 25 July 2022.

26 Pickard, Fisher and Gross, 'The think-tank laying the groundwork for a Labour government', *Financial Times*.

27 Pogrund and Yorke, 'The secretive guru who plotted Keir Starmer's path to power with undeclared cash', *Sunday Times*.

28 Pickard, Fisher and Gross, 'The think-tank laying the groundwork for a Labour government', *Financial Times*.

29 Pogrund and Yorke, 'The secretive guru who plotted Keir Starmer's path to power with undeclared cash', *Sunday Times*.

30 Parker and Pickard, 'Keir Starmer and big business, a love story', *Financial Times*.

31 Ned Simons, 'Labour Party Accepts 81 Voluntary Redundancies In Cost Cutting Drive', *Huffington Post*, 3 September 2021.

32 Alistair Gray, George Parker and Jim Pickard, 'Labour donor Dale Vince ordered to inform wife of future party funding,' *Financial Times*, 27 March 2024.

33 Parker and Pickard, 'Keir Starmer and big business, a love story', *Financial Times*.

34 Tony Thompson, 'How much money does Labour receive from the RMT and other trade unions?', Full Fact, 23 January 2023.

35 Ibid.

36 'The Labour Party: Financial statements for the year ended 31 December 2022', page 9, retrieved at https://search.electoralcommission.org.uk/Api/Accounts/Documents/25317 on 14 February 2024.

37 Parker and Pickard, 'Keir Starmer and big business, a love story', *Financial Times*.

38 Rowena Mason, 'Labour boosts election war chest with record quarter for funding', *Guardian*, 7 September 2023

39 Eleanor Langford, 'Labour left claims party conference has become 'corporate love-in'', inews.co.uk, 8 October 2023.

40 Tweet by Michael Crick on 8 October 2023, retrieved at https://x.com/MichaelLCrick/status/1710783718854361262?s=20

41 Rowena Mason and Aletha Adu, 'Donations to UK
    political parties nearly doubled to £93m in 2023',
    Guardian, 7 March 2024.

42 Jim Pickard and Michael O'Dwyer, 'Labour business
    day sells out in hours as executives woo Keir Starmer',
    Financial Times, 29 October 2023.

43 Parker and Pickard, 'Keir Starmer and big business, a love
    story', *Financial Times*

44 George Parker and Michael O'Dwyer, 'Tickets for Labour
    conference "business day" sold out in hours', *Financial
    Times*, 26 April 2024.

45 Tweet by Ian Fraser on 7 October 2023, retrieved at
    https://twitter.com/Ian_Fraser/status/
    1710763407522082900?s=20

46 Anna Gross and Jim Pickard, 'Labour quadruples use of
    consultants in run-up to UK election', *Financial Times*, 3
    January 2024.

47 Parker and Pickard, 'Keir Starmer and big business, a love
    story', *Financial Times*.

48 Kate Devlin and Adam Forrest, 'Scandal-hit Tory donor
    opens wallet to Starmer', *Independent*, 3 September 2023.

49 Will Hayward, 'Firm that bankrolled Vaughan Gething's
    campaign received £400k in loans of public money',
    Wales Online, 22 April 2024.

50 Tom Belger, 'Tories rake in almost five times more than
    Labour in recent donations', Labour List, 7 December
    2023.

7. What Is to be Done?

1   Barrington, 'There is more corruption and corruption
    risk in and around this government than any British
    government since 1945', LSE British Politics and Policy.

2   Billy Kenber, 'Revealed: Tory MP allegedly demanded

campaign cash to pay "bad people"', *The Times*, 18 April 2024.

3   Joint Strategic Needs Assessment Blackpool, 'Life expectancy', 30 January 2024.

4   Shelagh Parkinson, 'By-election candidates questioned over integrity as MPs conduct in the spotlight', *Blackpool Gazette*, 19 April 2024.

5   Valentina Romei, 'UK public trust in political parties collapses to 12%', *Financial Times*, 1 March 2024.

6   Labour, 'Only a changed Labour Party can get Britain's future back,' 5 January 2024.

7   Alix Culbertson, 'Boris Johnson's anti-corruption tsar resigns over partygate and will vote for PM to go', Sky News, 6 June 2022.

8   Peter Geoghegan, 'The parable of Britain's "anti-corruption champion"', Peter Geoghegan's Substack, 21 January 2024, received by email.

9   *The Economist*, 'Goodbye, good chap'.

10   Kiran Stacey, 'Keir Starmer pledges to clean up politics and crack down on cronyism', *Guardian*, 2 January 2024.

11   Simon Kuper, *Impossible City: Paris in the Twenty-First Century* (Profile Books, London, 2024), p. 191.

12   Xun Li, Wensi Pan, Gang Xu, 'A "leaner" government? The effect of China's anti-corruption campaign on the body weight and health of public sector employees', *Journal of Economic Behavior & Organization*, Volume 217, 2024, pp. 141–69.

13   Andrew Blick and Peter Hennessy, 'Good Chaps No More? Safeguarding the Constitution in Stressful Times' (The Constitution Society, London, 2019), p. 4.

14   Blick and Hennessy, *The Bonfire of the Decencies*, pp. 41–2.

15   Telegraph Obituaries, 'Sir John Bourn, Comptroller and

Auditor-General who enjoyed wielding his new powers – obituary', *Telegraph*, 27 November 2022.

16 Transparency International UK, 'Restoring Integrity in Public Life', June 2022.

17 Hodge, *Losing our moral compass.*

18 UK Governance Project, 'Our report', 1 February 2024.

19 Holmes, *Corruption,* p. 94.

20 Ibid., p. 126.

21 Quotes by Evans and Boo are from Speaker's Committee for the Independent Parliamentary Standards Authority, 'Oral evidence: Review of the Independent Parliamentary Standards Authority Corporate Plan 2017–18 and Main Estimate 2017–18', 28 March 2017.

22 House of Commons Public Administration and Constitutional Affairs Committee, 'Propriety of Governance in Light of Greensill', p. 16.

ACKNOWLEDGMENTS

I want to thank the Adam Smith Institute, Armando Castro, Deborah Crewe, Michael Crick, Ruth Evans, Matt Garrahan, Constantine Gonticas, Paul Gourd, Sergei Guriev, Paul Holden, Rana Mitter, Vadim Nikitin, George Parker, Peter Riddell, Darius Sanai, Robert Shrimsley, Ricardo Soares de Oliveira, Ed Smith, Ed Straw, Luke Tryl and Frank Vogl. There are many others who helped me with this book but who prefer to remain nameless.

Pamela Druckerman, Pauline Harris and Adam Kuper read the manuscript and weeded out some of the mistakes.

At the *Financial Times Weekend*, I want to thank my colleagues Janine Gibson, Matt Vella, Neil O'Sullivan, Cordelia Jenkins, Anthony Lavelle, Cherish Rufus and Andrea Crisp.

Thanks to Andrew Franklin, Valentina Zanca, Penny Daniel, Rosie Parnham, Georgia Poplett and all the others at my marvellous publisher, Profile.

Thanks to my trusted agents Gordon Wise and Elliot Prior at Curtis Brown.

And thanks above all to Pamela Druckerman for somehow, most of the time, tolerating me and my books.

SELECT BIBLIOGRAPHY

Books

Tim Bale, *The Conservative Party after Brexit: Turmoil and Transformation* (Polity Press, Cambridge, 2023)

Catherine Belton, *Putin's People: How the KGB Took Back Russia and Then Took on the West* (William Collins, London, 2021)

Andrew Blick and Peter Hennessy, *The Bonfire of the Decencies: Repairing and Restoring the British Constitution* (Haus Publishing, London, 2022)

Tom Bower, *Broken Vows: Tony Blair, The Tragedy of Power* (Faber & Faber, London, 2016)

John Bowers, *Downward Spiral: Collapsing public standards and how to restore them* (Manchester University Press, Manchester, 2024)

Chris Bryant, *Code of Conduct: Why We Need to Fix Parliament – and How to Do It* (Bloomsbury, London, 2023)

Oliver Bullough, *Butler to the World: How Britain Became the Servant of Tycoons, Tax Dodgers, Kleptocrats and Criminals* (Profile, London, 2022)

Tom Burgis, *Cuckooland: Where the Rich Own the Truth* (William Collins, London, 2024)

Julia Cagé, *Le prix de la démocratie* (Gallimard, Paris, 2022)

Stefan Dercon, *Gambling on Development: Why Some Countries Win and Others Lose* (Hurst, London, 2022)

Ian Dunt, *How Westminster Works ... and Why It Doesn't* (Weidenfeld & Nicholson, London, 2023, uncorrected proof)

Peter Geoghegan, *Democracy For Sale: Dark Money and Dirty Politics* (Head of Zeus, London, 2021)

Leslie Holmes, *Corruption: A Very Short Introduction* (Oxford University Press, Oxford, 2015)

Ian Kennedy, *Cleaning up the Mess: After the MPs' Expenses Scandal* (Biteback, London, 2019)

Jolyon Maugham, *Bringing Down Goliath* (WH Allen, London, 2023)

Duncan Mavin, *Pyramid of Lies: The Prime Minister, the Banker and the Billion-Pound Scandal* (Pan Books, London, 2023)

Avner Offer, *Understanding the Private-Public Divide: Markets, Governments, and Time Horizons* (Cambridge University Press, Cambridge, 2022)

Matthew Parris, *Great Parliamentary Scandals: Four Centuries of Calumny, Smear & Innuendo* (Robson Books, London, 1997)

Arthur Snell, *How Britain Broke the World: War, Greed and Blunders from Kosovo to Afghanistan, 1997–2022* (Canbury Press, Kingston upon Thames, 2022)

Ed Straw, *Stand & Deliver: A Design for Successful Government* (Treaty for Government, York, 2014)

Geoffrey Wheatcroft, *The Strange Death of Tory England* (Allen Lane, London, 2005)

Articles and reports

Committee on Standards in Public Life, 'Political party finance: ending the big donor culture' (November 2011)

Mirko Draca, Colin Green and Swarnodeep Homroy, 'Financing UK democracy: A stocktake of 20 years of political donations', CAGE working paper no. 642, November 2022

Select Bibliography

Jess Garland, 'Deal or No Deal: How to put an end to party funding scandals', Electoral Reform Society, February 2015

John Heathershaw, Alexander Cooley, Tom Mayne, Casey Michel, Tena Prelec, Jason Sharman and Ricardo Soares de Oliveira, 'The UK's kleptocracy problem: How servicing post-Soviet elites weakens the rule of law', Chatham House, Russia and Eurasia Programme, December 2021

Peter Hennessy, 'Harvesting the Cupboards': Why Britain Has Produced No Administrative Theory or Ideology in the Twentieth Century (Transactions of the Royal Historical Society, Vol. 4 (1994)

House of Commons Committee of Privileges, 'Matter referred on 21 April 2022 (conduct of Rt Hon Boris Johnson): Final Report', June 15, 2023

House of Commons Public Administration and Constitutional Affairs Committee, 'Propriety of Governance in Light of Greensill: Fourth Report of Session 2022-23', November 29, 2022

Margaret Hodge, *Losing our moral compass: Corrupt money and corrupt politics* (APPG on Anti-Corruption & Responsible Tax, June 2023)

Intelligence and Security Committee of Parliament, 'Russia', July 21, 2020

Transparency International UK, 'Position Paper: Managing Revolving Door Risks in Westminster', March 2023

Transparency International UK, 'Track and trace: Identifying corruption risks in UK public procurement for the covid-19 pandemic', April 2021

INDEX

Index

Index

Index

Index

Index

Index